TEN QUESTIONS GOD ASKED

TEN QUESTIONS GOD ASKED

MICHELE ARMSTRONG

© 2010 by Michele Armstrong. All rights reserved.

Pleasant Word (a division of WinePress Publishing, PO Box 428, Enumclaw, WA 98022) functions only as book publisher. As such, the ultimate design, content, editorial accuracy, and views expressed or implied in this work are those of the author.

No part of this publication may be reproduced, stored in a retrieval system, or transmitted in any way by any means—electronic, mechanical, photocopy, recording, or otherwise—without the prior permission of the copyright holder, except as provided by USA copyright law.

Unless otherwise noted, all Scriptures are taken from the *New American Standard Bible*, © 1960, 1963, 1968, 1971, 1972, 1973, 1975, 1977 by The Lockman Foundation. Used by permission.

Scripture references marked NLT are taken from the *Holy Bible, New Living Translation*, copyright © 1996, 2004 by Tyndale Charitable Trust. Used by permission of Tyndale House Publishers, Wheaton, Illinois 60189. All rights reserved.

ISBN 13: 978-1-4141-1729-4
ISBN 10: 1-4141-1729-9
Library of Congress Catalog Card Number: 2010902002

To my parents, mentors, friends
~Woody and Helen Armstrong~
thank you

CONTENTS

Introduction xi

For the Reader xv

Question #1: Genesis 3:9— "Where Are You?" 1
After Adam and Eve had eaten the fruit, they heard the sound of God walking in the garden, so they hid in the bushes. "Then the Lord God called to the man and said to him, 'Where are you?'"

Question #2: Genesis 4:6— "Why Are You Angry?" 13
Cain's sacrifice was not acceptable to God, so Cain sulked. "Then the Lord said to Cain, 'Why are you angry? And why has your countenance fallen?'"

Question #3: 1 Kings 19:9— "What Are You Doing Here?" ... 25
Elijah had just incurred the wrath of Queen Jezebel, so he ran and hid in the wilderness. "...And behold, the word of the Lord came to him and He said to him, 'What are you doing here, Elijah?'"

Question #4: Job 38:1–2— "Who Is This that Darkens Counsel by Words Without Knowledge?" 37

Job had been crying out to God for vindication and an explanation for his intense suffering. "Then the Lord answered Job out of the whirlwind and said, 'Who is this that darkens counsel by words without knowledge?'"

Question #5: Matthew 9:28— "Do You Believe I Am Able to Do This?" 51

Two blind men were following Jesus, wanting Him to heal them. "When He entered the house, the blind men came up to Him and He said to them, 'Do you believe I am able to do this?'"

Question #6: Mark 8:29— "Who Do You Say that I Am?" 61

Jesus questioned the disciples about what others thought of Him and then what they thought of Him. "And He continued by questioning them, 'But who do you say that I am?'"

Question #7: Luke 24:17— "What Are You Discussing Together as You Walk Along?" 73

Two men were walking and talking about all the events concerning Jesus, when suddenly the resurrected Jesus joined them, but they did not recognize Him. "He asked them, 'What are you discussing together as you walk along?'"

Question #8: John 1:38— "What Do You Seek?" 85

Two men began to follow Jesus after John called Him, the "Lamb of God." "And Jesus turned and saw them following and said to them, 'What do you seek?'"

Question #9: John 6:67— "You Do Not Want to Go Away Also, Do You?" 97

Jesus had just preached some difficult teachings, and several followers left, unable to accept it. "So Jesus said to the twelve, 'You do not want to go away also, do you?'"

Question #10: Acts 9:4— "Why Are You Persecuting Me?" . . 109
> *Saul was on his way to Damascus to persecute more Christians when Jesus appeared to him. "As he [Saul] was traveling...suddenly a light from heaven flashed around him and he fell to the ground and heard a voice saying of him, 'Saul, Saul, Why are you persecuting Me?'"*

Endnotes 123

Bibliography 127

INTRODUCTION

FOR THE PAST several years I have been an elementary school teacher in my hometown. This experience, like most experiences with children, has taught me many things about God's relationship with us. I have always thought of God as my Teacher and Counselor, and being a teacher myself has reinforced this impression.

As a teacher, I realize the importance of asking the right questions of my students at the right time. Certain types of questions require the student to simply remember the information that I just said. This is a test of knowledge. In a lesson about the solar system I might ask, "What are the names of the planets?" and the students will respond by repeating what they just heard from me.

However, once I know the students have the basic knowledge, I need to ask different questions rather than just going to the next topic. After they can tell me the names of the planets in order, I might ask why Pluto is so much colder than Earth or why the sun and moon appear to be the same size, when we know that the sun is so much larger. I've learned the importance of asking these kinds of questions (only after they have a knowledge foundation) because it forces the students to think more critically. Rarely will they make these connections on their own; I, their teacher, must guide them.

As we relate to God, it is much in the same way. Like the Scriptures say, He will discipline us and instruct us, yet He will not give us more than we can bear (1 Cor. 10:13). He teaches us through His Word and through our experiences, but there also comes a time of questioning. It is through asking and answering questions that God helps us to make connections between His Word (Truth) and our lives. Just as I question my students in order to make them stop and analyze the information I have just told them, God questions His children for the same purpose. Our knowledge of the Word is void if we cannot make the connection to our everyday lives. The Truth that is revealed must shed light on experience, and experience can only gain meaning and cohesiveness when examined through the Truth.

From the moment sin entered the world, God has been bringing humankind back to Himself. He has spoken like thunder and whispered like the wind; He has stirred the waters and calmed them; He has shaken the mountains and given visions and dreams. God has used these and many other avenues to teach and guide those willing to listen and see. And God is ever personal. As I have read through the biblical accounts and examined God's dealings with those He loves, it is evident that He is never more personal, more direct, more piercing than when He is asking a question. Since God does not question us so that we become informed, He must question us so that we will grow.

The ten questions I have chosen are obviously not an exhaustive collection, nor do they represent all the types of questions that God has asked. I chose these ten because they have been asked of me at one point or another. And as I was writing, I found that several themes were recurring and intertwined: trust, discipline, love, mercy, holiness, and faith. Any question from God inevitably will be tied to aspects of His character and to human nature, and to the comparing and contrasting of the two.

Another thing to note about these questions is that they are not rhetorical (with the possible exception of the one asked of Job), but they require deeper reflection than we might first have imagined.

Lastly, the instances I have chosen demonstrate God's dealings with the righteous (with the possible exception of Cain). It would be a whole other venture to examine how or if God questions the wicked.

My purpose in writing this book was simply for Christians to know and understand God more fully. This may seem too ambiguous or generic, but consider the outcome. If we understand who God is (that is, His character), then we will begin to understand all other matters of life, because life centers on the One who created it. By our examining how God relates to His people, and specifically how He questions us, God gives us yet another glimpse of Himself.

Essentially, God asks these questions for two reasons: He is holy, and He is love. His holiness requires that we be changed, and it is by His love that the change takes place. Though His questions might at times sound like a mother soothing her child or like thunder speaking to an ant, they are always out of His love and holiness, for the purpose of bringing us back to Himself.

It is my desire and aim to use as much Scripture as possible for my own accountability and for the readers'. I encourage the reader to look up each reference and read the entire passage within its context in order to gain fuller understanding. I mainly reference the *New American Standard Bible* when quoting Scripture, unless otherwise noted. All the italics in the quoted passages were added by me for emphasis or to point out the connection between the discussion and the Scripture.

It should be understood that I wrote under the assumption that the Bible is the infallible word of God and that "all Scripture is inspired by God and profitable for teaching, for reproof, for correction, for training in righteousness…" (2 Tim. 3:16). The Bible is not some ethereal book of platitudes; it is real and true for each one of us in our personal lives, in how we see ourselves, and in our relationships with God and other people. Ultimately, the Bible is God's revelation of Himself, through which we have redemption. And a life devoted to understanding and living out God's revelation will not be in vain.

December 2004

FOR THE READER

AS WITH MOST books, this book was written with a specific audience in mind: Christians. That is not to exclude any readers who feel they do not fit this description or who are not sure that they do. I only state this to make my intentions clear that this book is written for those who are dedicated to Christ, to becoming more like Him, and to working out their salvation in fear and trembling. It is my hope that in this age there will be a renewal of such dedication, starting in my own heart and mind.

On a more pragmatic note, I wanted to give a brief comment about the format of the chapters. Each of the ten chapters is divided into three sections: 1) Context, 2) Digging Deeper, and 3) Reflections and Conclusion. This format was designed to fit the individual reader or a group.

1. **Context:** This section discusses the Scripture surrounding the question. Any verse must be examined within the context in which it appears for its meaning to be truly understood. The context of a passage can be further studied

by reading the broader context: the context of a verse is found in the paragraph, the context of the paragraph is the chapter (roughly), the context of the chapter is the book (for example, Genesis), and the context of the book is the entire Bible. For insight into the history, culture, and language, refer to a commentary dealing with the passage in question.

2. **Digging Deeper:** As the writer of Hebrews stated so poignantly, "The word of God is living and active" (4:12)—as opposed to being static and irrelevant. If you have been a Christian for a while and have read much of the Bible, perhaps you are already familiar with many of the verses or questions that are in this book. However, I challenge you not to assume you have gleaned all possible meaning from these verses and their contexts. By all means, you will not have done that after reading this book. I simply mean that God constantly wants us to go deeper, beyond the elementary teachings of the Word, toward the more challenging but necessary lessons of humility, joy in suffering, patience, and compassion. As you dig deeper into the gold mine of His Word, you will find that the real treasure lies further in.

3. **Conclusion and Reflection:** The questions in this section are intended as a jumping-off point for further meditation on the relevant passage. Be open to the possibility that God may lead you to reflect on some other point. If you are in a group, understand that whatever you share could be used by God to encourage another person. Whether you are alone or with others, God's intent is for you to know Him as He is and be changed as a result. I want to encourage you to take the reflection time seriously and be willing to share with someone. This makes any decisions for change more real and makes you accountable to another person.

It is crucial for Christians today to be equipped for the challenges ahead. The world around us scarcely believes in objective truth, much less the Bible or the God described therein. So Christian, read your Bible, but don't just read it—you must believe it and be able to discuss why. And don't just believe or explain it; you and I must live it in such a way that the people around us are convinced and convicted by the truth of God.

QUESTION #1

GENESIS 3:9— "WHERE ARE YOU?"

> Just for the sake of discussion, I could pretend that this is a fence, a limitation, a boundary. A boundary I crossed over, and shouldn't have.[1]
>
> —from *Piercing the Darkness*

THE FIRST WORDS God spoke to Adam after the fall were in the form of a simple question: "Then the Lord called to the man and said to him, 'Where are you?'" It seems strange that God would choose to ask this question. I might have asked why they ate the fruit or what they were thinking. In a way, the question is almost childlike, as if it were some tragic game of hide-and-seek. Ironically, this analogy is not far from the truth.

Context

In Chapter 3:1–5, the serpent converses with Eve about eating the fruit that God had forbidden to her and Adam. By verse 6, she is convinced to eat it and then gives some to Adam. Suddenly aware of their nakedness, they fashion coverings out of leaves. When they hear the sound of the Lord walking in the garden, they hide behind the trees (3:7–8).

Genesis 3:7 is key to understanding this passage and God's first question: "Then the eyes of both of them were opened, and they knew that they were naked..." Note the contrast with their previous state in Genesis 2:25: "And the man and his wife were both naked and were *not* ashamed." For the first time in human history, there is an experience of fear and shame, and from this moment on these two emotions begin to reign in human hearts.

Notice the order of the events. First, Eve decided it was a good idea to disobey God. She assumed God was keeping something good from her, and she thought that she could (and must) attain it on her own. She became a usurper. Call it pride, self-centeredness, unbelief; by whatever name it is called, it is just as foul. In that instant, Eve broke away from God's original design. Only then did shame, guilt, and fear become a part of the human experience. Our sin is rooted in our pride in thinking that somehow we can do better than God. This sin separates us from God, and being separated from God is unnatural for us. In this unnatural state, we experience shame, guilt, and fear. By Genesis 6 the people of the earth had become so evil that God sought to destroy them all, except for one family. Then in chapter 11, the people were once again completely ignorant of God and how to relate to Him. These first 11 chapters of Genesis describe the human condition: we are created in God's image, separated from Him by sin, and in need of redemption.

Digging Deeper

Shame comes when we have an awareness or perception of too much exposure, whether physical, emotional, or social. It's like that dream that everyone has of being naked, or not having enough clothing, while standing in front of a crowd. We have these kinds of dreams when we are anxious or feeling vulnerable. What is your instinct when you feel this kind of shame, waking or dreaming? Hide. Find the fastest route out of the situation; find something to cover yourself; do whatever it takes to ease the sense of shame.

Although we avoid and hate those shameful situations, how much worse it is to have no sense of shame in our sinful state. Those who are unaware of any shame or feel no guilt are frightful outcasts. The most common label for this kind of person in modern society is "sociopath" or "psychopath."

But what about the one who is unaware only in certain areas? What happens when our sense of shame is *gradually* deadened and we no longer feel exposed? Jeremiah 8 records God's lament and rebuke of His people who have turned away from Him. They no longer looked to God as a measure of moral standard and so felt no shame in blatantly disregarding the sacred covenant relationship. In 8:12 it is especially relevant: "Were they ashamed because of the abominations they had done? They certainly were not ashamed. *And they did not know how to blush.*" First Timothy 4:1–2 is a similar warning, stating that the time will come when people will "abandon the faith and follow deceiving spirits and things taught by demons. Such teachings come through hypocritical liars, whose *consciences have been seared* as with a hot iron." The people were no longer embarrassed by anything they did; nothing was shameful.

This did not take place overnight. It has been said that a toad placed in room temperature water can be boiled alive because it does not sense the gradual increase in the water's temperature. Think about American society over the past one hundred years. Things that were not even discussed in public before are now graphically portrayed in every facet of the media. It seems that it is our society's mission to reduce or numb our sense of shame. Ironically, the only real shame has become shame itself. Our culture teaches us to embrace and flaunt who we are, to be proud and unapologetic.

It says, "Whatever you do, don't feel ashamed about who you are, what you have done, or what you desire to do."

Yet it is proper that we feel shame, for we have sinned against a holy God. Remove the holy God, and you will remove the shame. This sounds like a tempting option, and many gladly subscribe to it, but they have not thought through to the logical end. Ephesians 4:17–19 tells us what happens to those who attempt to remove God in order to squelch their shame. Paul says that these people have been "darkened in their understanding, excluded from the life of God because of the ignorance that is in them because of the hardness of their heart; and they, having become callous, have given themselves over to sensuality *for the practice of every kind of impurity* with greediness." They have done away with God and in turn become calloused, unable to sense proper boundaries, and so they practice *every kind* of impurity.

Stephen King's book *The Stand* is an epic story about God's judgment on human society. He poignantly summarizes the reasons for this judgment:

> Shall I tell you what sociology teaches us about the human race? I'll give it to you in a nutshell. Show me a man or woman alone and I'll show you a saint. Give me two and they'll fall in love. Give me three and they'll reinvent the charming thing we call "society." Give me four and they'll build a pyramid. Give me five and they'll make one an outcast. Give me six and they'll reinvent prejudice. Give me seven and in seven years they'll reinvent warfare.[2]

To test the truth of this, just read Genesis 1–11. It's astonishing how quickly humanity degenerates to murder, violence, boasting, drunkenness, and idol worship. Despite this, God is not without compassion, even in the midst of judgment. The very fact that God sent prophets to warn His people is a demonstration of His love for them.

God's love is like a vast spectrum, and each point on the spectrum is a specific way that God manifests His love. The "Father" love of God is at each end of the spectrum, representing two extremes. The one extreme is summarized in the statement God made to Adam in Genesis 2:18: "If you eat from the tree, you will surely die." God sets boundaries and limitations because of His love for us and so that we might demonstrate our love to Him. The existence of boundaries also implies that there are consequences for violating them, since without consequences, any boundary becomes meaningless. At the other end of the spectrum, the demonstration of God's love is made complete by the cross. On the one hand God said, "You will surely die," while on the other God leaned in further and said to us, "I will die in your place." Like any good father, God the Father has set limitations and consequences, but when the consequence meant eternal separation from Him, our Father stepped in to pay the price of death.

To appreciate this love that the Father has bestowed on us, we must first understand our guilt. It is appropriate to distinguish between shame and guilt, since many might think that these words are synonymous. Shame is what we feel or sense when we are aware of our own guilt. Adam and Eve felt ashamed because they knew they were guilty. Children look down at the ground in shame when they are caught coloring on the wall. Shame is merely a state of mind or heart and is only helpful to the extent that it lines up with the truth. The mother who unknowingly passes on a genetic defect to her child may feel a false sense of shame, even though she is not guilty. Conversely, sociopaths feel no shame, though they may be guilty of the worst crimes.

Guilt is an objective reality that does not come and go whether or not we feel ashamed. One popular writer of Christian fiction, Frank Peretti, captures this in his book *Piercing the Darkness*. The main character struggles with guilt over the intentional drowning of her baby girl. She had numbed the shame by denying God and blaming her "spirit guide," who is actually a demon. In a pivotal scene, she revisits the very bathroom where she drowned her baby. As she sits by the tub, she ponders the possibility of her own guilt. "Just for the sake of discussion, I could pretend that this [the side of the tub] is a fence, a limitation, a boundary. A boundary I crossed over, and shouldn't have."[3] She battles with the concept of absolute truth versus moral relativism, but finally decides she would rather say she did something wrong. "Why? Because I need a fence. Even if I'm on the wrong side of it, I need a fence."[4]

This is such a powerful picture of our need for boundaries and the danger of proclaiming our own guiltlessness. Most of us would feel confident in saying that killing a child is wrong, but that is now. It used to be that abortion was considered wrong, both on moral and legal grounds. Is it now morally right to abort unborn children since the law allows it? How long will it be before pedophilia is allowed and even approved by our society, much like it was in ancient Greece? If there are no moral absolutes, then nothing is absolutely wrong and there can be no real guilt in our own estimation. According to society, our guilt is at best temporary and arbitrary, but if there are absolutes, there must be guilt.

Adam and Eve were given an absolute. They were told they must not eat of the Tree of Knowledge of Good and Evil, but they willfully disobeyed and became guilty. They crossed a boundary that should not have been crossed and felt properly ashamed.

Then we come to God's question, which now might seem more appropriate. "Where are you?" is often a question of spiritual location. When He asked this question, God must have been greatly pained, for He knew the man and woman had separated themselves from Him. God recognized that the man was not where he usually was, and He wanted Adam to be aware of this change also. God asked Adam where he was not because He didn't know or couldn't see where Adam was hiding; God asked the question to make Adam aware of what he was doing and why. God asked the question to let Adam know he had stepped over a boundary. We can tell by Adam's response in verse 10 that this was the case. He admits, "I heard the sound of You in the garden, and I was afraid because I was naked; so I hid myself."

Fear is at the center of nearly all negative emotions. It has been said that to be alive is to be fearful. Ultimately, we fear our own death and destruction. You could even say that our shame is rooted in fear; when you feel ashamed it is because you fear some kind of punishment or negative outcome, such as ridicule, isolation, condemnation, or even death. In our fear we begin to weave our own version of reality. Look at Adam's response again: "I was afraid because I was naked." But Adam had always been naked, so why was he suddenly so afraid? In reality, Adam's fear wasn't because he was naked per se, but because of the disobedience that led to his awareness of his nakedness. He did not confess his disobedience, but rather he cast the blame on his wife, who in turn blamed the serpent. They were fearful of God's retribution, and rightly so.

My personal experience with this question is often in the midst of my fear and self-pity. I become fearful of the future and feel sorry for myself because I am not somewhere else, somewhere further along, or somewhere better. In these times I take deliberate steps away from the narrow road and find it difficult to get back. Just like Adam, I want to blame others or the circumstances, but instead of helping, this response only takes me further away from God. During these times, I feel as though I become a spectator instead of a participant in my own life. In a recent struggle over this very issue, I realized that I did not want to be on the sidelines, only watching and hearing of others living a life devoted to God. "Where are you, Michele?" God, ever the Gentleman, beckons me back to the place I left. I am ashamed sometimes at how long it takes me to hear this question. I am learning to be quicker in noticing where I stand in my spiritual life. Every moment counts. I don't want to miss the abundant life God has promised to those who follow Him.

When God asks us where we are, like with Adam, it is not so much our physical location that is the point, but rather our spiritual location. "Where are you? For you have gone from Me," God asks. Just as Adam did, you must then take note of your location. Stand up and look around. Where have you gone in your attempt to hide from an omnipresent God? It might seem silly that Adam and Eve thought they could hide from God by going behind some bushes. But it was only another indication of their fallen nature, for they no longer understood God as they once did. Whereas before they did not even desire to hide or conceive of hiding from God, now they not only desired it but also thought it was possible. If God does indeed exist, then we must hide from Him, for He is holy and we are not. The only problem is that we cannot hide (see Psalm 139:1–12). It is like the nightmare of being overexposed in front of crowd, but much worse because it is real. What a fearful thing it would be to fall into the hands of the living God (Heb. 10:31). Strangely, God did not incinerate the couple hiding in the brush, nor did He ridicule them; instead, He asked them where they were.

Something must be done about the guilt that we have heaped on ourselves. Shall we do good deeds to compensate for every evil deed we do? If we jump high enough and hard enough, can we ever tip the scales in our favor? The answer is no. In fact, it seems that the more you try to earn your redemption, the further you stray from it. The idea of earning our redemption, our freedom from guilt, is one of the most arrogant thoughts we can have. The only thought more arrogant is to say that God does not exist at all. "The *fool* says in his heart 'There is no God'" (Ps. 14:1a). When I think that I can buy my own justification, I believe two lies: 1) my sin is not that bad, and 2) God is not that holy. Truthfully, our sin *is* that bad, and God *is* that holy. There is no small separation between God and man. When God calls out, "Where are you?" it rings out across an infinite divide as a reminder of how far our sin removes us from God.

Isaiah 6:1–7 offers a summary of the major biblical themes: God's holiness, human sin, and God's act of redemption. In these verses Isaiah recorded a vision he saw of the Lord in His throne room. He writes, "I saw the Lord sitting on a throne, lofty and exalted, with the train of His robe filling the temple…And one [seraphim] called out to another and said, 'Holy, Holy, Holy is the Lord of hosts, The whole earth is full of His glory.'" The first four verses establish the holiness of God. He is lofty, exalted, and worthy to be worshiped. As Isaiah looks on this scene, he becomes aware of himself. He cries out, "Woe to me, for I am undone! Because I am a man of unclean lips, and I live among a people of unclean lips; For my eyes have seen the King, the Lord of hosts." Our sin doesn't seem so wrong until it is laid up against the one who is Right. Since I cannot earn my redemption (and redemption is a necessity), what can be done? God, in His infinite wisdom, saw fit to provide a way. Isaiah 6:6–7 is a beautiful picture of redemption. Isaiah's iniquity was taken away and his sins were atoned for by the fire of the altar touching his mouth. Imagine Isaiah's relief, knowing that the alternative would have been death.

This passage in Isaiah isn't the first biblical account of God's redemptive action. No sooner did the man and woman become guilty than God revealed His plan for our redemption. Genesis 3:15 is often recognized as a messianic prophecy, looking forward to the time that the Son of God would come and die in order to save us from our sin, only to be raised again so that the sting of death might be removed. Like a gun without bullets, death no longer holds the threat it once did. We can be free from fear. "There is no fear in love; but perfect love cast out fear, because fear involves punishment, and the one who fears is not perfected in love" (1 John 4:18). For those who have believed in their guilt before a holy God, and believed even more that God has poured out His grace, there is no longer any fear or shame. God calls, "Come to Me, all who are weary and heavy-laden, and I will give you rest" (Matt. 11:28). "Where are you? For you have gone from Me, and I want to show you the way back." We must be aware of and admit our guilt because it is real, but we are not condemned to suffer the consequences forever, even if there must be some suffering now. His grace is even greater than our guilt.

God wants to restore the relationship with us for which we were designed. This relationship is the only way back to our true humanity. Ironically, we often say things like, "I'm only human," as though it excuses or explains some failure or sin. The truth is, if we were "only" or simply human we would not desire sin at all, but we would run away from it as quickly as possible. If we were truly human we would seek God and be in relationship with Him, for this is true humanity. Our sin has made us a shadowy version of humanity—so much so that we have redefined what being human really means. Adam and Eve not only lost fellowship with God, but also with themselves. Those who lose themselves forget that they are lost.

As you think of times that God might have asked, "Where are you?" do you come across times that you asked that same question of God? This is a popular question that people, believers and nonbelievers alike, ask. Usually we ask this during times of pain and suffering. I usually ask this when I think God does not care, has gone away, or does not even exist because my pain doesn't seem consistent with His existence or presence. This is what C. S. Lewis called "the problem of pain," which is also the title of one of his books. I will not attempt to tackle the problem of pain and suffering here. There are many who have already written excellent books on this topic. But I will point out that given our long history of asking God, "Where are You?" it is interesting to see that God asked it first. It is *we* who do the leaving, not God. Before you ever asked God where He was, He asked you the same question. His answer to your question is bound to how you answer His.

James 4:8a instructs us to "Draw near to God and He will draw near to you." In Acts 17:22–31 Paul delivers a powerful sermon, testifying that God created mankind "that they would seek God, if perhaps they might grope for Him and find Him, though He is not far from each of us; for in Him we live and move and exist." And Jesus promises in Matthew 28:20 "I am with you always, even to the end of the age."

Conclusion and Reflection

Where is God? He is not far from you, no matter how far your heart may be from Him. God's answer is constant, just as He is constant. But you must answer His question: "Where are you?" This question can only be answered through careful examination.

- Does the place where you are (physically and spiritually) reflect the beliefs you profess?
- Do the beliefs you profess reflect the truth revealed in the Bible?
- In what ways do you attempt to hide from God by minimizing your sin or diminishing God's holiness? Are you blaming others or even God for your situation?
- How much do you rely on your feelings of shame to determine whether or not you are guilty?
- In what areas have you allowed your sense of shame to become deadened?

God will shed light on your location so that you can find the way back. Just ask.

QUESTION #2

GENESIS 4:6— "WHY ARE YOU ANGRY?"

> "The very first tear he made was so deep that I thought it had gone right into my heart. And when he began pulling the skin off, it hurt worse than anything I've ever felt."[5]
> —from *Voyage of the Dawn Treader*

THE MOST STRIKING thing about God's entire interaction with Cain in Genesis 4 is that God knew beforehand that Cain would not listen. Why would God try to intervene when He knew it would not change Cain's actions? The very fact that God bothered to ask this question is worth examining. It tells us something about the character of God, which is a theme throughout all of Scripture.

Context

Ezekiel 3 has come up more than once in my life. In these verses God instructs the prophet Ezekiel to go to the exiled Israelites. This is not unusual because God repeatedly sent messengers to deliver warnings. However, in this instance with Ezekiel, God tells him that "the house of Israel will not be willing to listen to you, since they are not willing to listen to Me" (3:7). God already knew that the people would not listen and would even be hostile, yet He sends the prophet anyway. In Ezekiel 3:8 God promises Ezekiel that He will make his "face as hard as their faces and your forehead as hard as their foreheads." In other words, God would make Ezekiel just as stubborn in delivering the message as the people would be not listening to it.

Other instances of God extending rejected mercy occur throughout the Bible. One of the most dramatic examples is during Israel's exodus from Egypt. God sends warning after warning to the pharaoh, yet he continues to harden his heart and ignore God's signs. Isaiah 45:5b records God's words: "I will strengthen you though you have not acknowledged Me." Paul also states the matter very plainly in Romans 5:8: "…while we were yet sinners, Christ died for us." Time and again God gives the sinner a chance to repent and be saved, even when God already knows this chance will be rejected.

What does this say about God? What kind of God attempts to reach out to people whom He knows will reject, hate, and even curse Him? Most people would say that it is because God loves us, but they would be only partially right. The full answer is found in Isaiah 48:8–11, where God speaks to Israel:

> I knew that you would deal very treacherously; and you have been called a rebel from birth. *For the sake of My name* I delay My wrath, and *for My praise* I restrain it for you, in order not to cut you off….. *For My own sake*, I will act; For how can My name be profaned? And *My glory I will not give to another.*

God does not love us because we are worthy or lovable but for the sake of His own name and glory. God is sending a message about Himself, not just to mankind, but to every corner of the universe. His question to Cain in spite of his rebelliousness is like a billboard to the universe declaring God's love and mercy so that God might be recognized for who He is. God does what He does, in His way and in His time, for the sake of His own glory.

So this Creator-God of the universe, who is a consuming fire, concerned with His renown, comes down one day to ask a man why he is angry and depressed. Some context is helpful to understand exactly what happened and why Cain is angry in the first place. In Genesis 4:1–2 we learn that Eve gave birth to two sons, Cain and Abel. Cain worked the ground, and Abel raised animals. When it came time to bring a sacrifice before God, Abel brings an animal (4:4) and Cain brings "the fruit of the ground" (4:3). Genesis 4:4b–5 says that God has regard or favor for Abel's offering but not for Cain's. The passage is not explicit in telling us why, but Hebrews 11:4 says that it was "by faith that Abel brought a better sacrifice than Cain." Also, Genesis 4:4 states that Abel's sacrifice is "of the firstlings of his flock and of their fat portions," which is considered the best for sacrifice.

It can be generally understood then that Cain *knowingly* does not bring an acceptable sacrifice. It would be interesting to know how God expressed His disfavor, but those details are also left out. All we know is that "Cain became very angry and his countenance fell" (4:6). Now we come to God's question: "Why are you angry? And why has your countenance fallen?" (4:6). God almost sounds like a counselor here, which is not inappropriate. God shows Himself to be deeply concerned and invested in people's lives. Yet Cain responds to God's questions and warning by killing his brother in cold blood.

Digging Deeper

Has God ever asked you, or have you ever asked yourself, why you were angry or depressed? Anger and dejection are rooted in fear. In our sinful state, we typically feel angry when we are threatened in some way. Think about the last time you were angry. Most likely it was because someone or something seemed threatening, causing you to feel shamed or powerless. Usually our anger flares when we sense that we must protect ourselves, either physically or emotionally. In these precarious times, some people might cling to their fear or shame, but others will turn to anger. This is a more attractive alternative to many people because they feel that anger gives them back some control. Rather than giving a rude person the satisfaction of seeing you back down in fear or embarrassment, you lash out in anger in an attempt to regain your lost dignity.

We are capable of living lives defined by anger in an effort to control the situations and people that surround us. Depression is only a passive kind of anger, for it is rooted in the same thing, just expressed differently. Depression is another attempt to gain control by resenting that control has been lost. The problem is, of course, that you are far from being in control. You are a slave.

It would seem that anger itself must be a horrific sin, but this is not necessarily true. When we use anger in an effort to defend our own honor, it is sinful, but this doesn't have to always be the case. Ephesians 4:26 is often quoted in discussions of anger: "Be angry and yet do not sin." The word "sin" here means "to miss the mark," as in archery. It's like the arrow that missed the bull's eye or missed the target altogether. In effect, Paul is telling us to be angry, but in your anger *make sure you hit the mark.*

Cain became angry, but he missed the mark. Cain directed his anger toward his brother Abel (who had done him no wrong) and ended up killing him (4:8). Cain couldn't see that his anger was with God. There is no record of Cain responding at all to God's questions or warnings. Though Cain would not have hit the bull's eye had he directed his anger toward God, I believe he would have hit the target, and maybe eventually reached the center.

God was actually doing Cain a favor by disapproving of his sacrifice. God was trying to teach Cain how to relate to Him and approach Him: Yahweh must be regarded as a holy God. I don't blame Cain for not receiving this message, because I miss it too. The truth is, God uses and allows discomfort in our lives in order to spark a conversation. How easy it is to reject pain as a messenger from God! Cain certainly did. Yet God places the coffee table in the dark living room of our lives that we might bang our shins on it and stop in our tracks to yell out, "Why is this here?" God is not offended at such a question because the alternative is silence. In silence towards God you will soon find that you are capable of the most grievous sins. They are not as far from you or me as we would like to think.

It is ridiculous when Christians talk about how people shouldn't express anger towards God, as if God didn't know that those thoughts were already in our hearts. Even more ludicrous is to think that God would rather we fain praise and worship while harboring the unsightly emotions of fear, anger, and depression inside. There is no record of anyone being condemned for expressing these things towards God. We are only condemned when we are unwilling to move from them.

The Psalms are filled with the ravings of the angry and depressed: "O Lord, how my adversaries have increased! Many are rising up against me" (3:1). "Give ear to my words, O Lord, consider my groaning" (5:1). "Be gracious to me, O Lord, for I am pining away; Heal me, O Lord, for my bones are dismayed and my soul is greatly dismayed…I am weary with my sighing…I dissolve my couch with tears. My eye has wasted away with grief" (6:2–7). "Why do You stand afar off, O Lord? Why do you hide in times of trouble?" (10:1). "How long, O Lord? Will You forget me forever? How long will You hide Your face from me? How long shall I take counsel in my soul, having sorrow in my heart all the day? How long will my enemy be exalted over me?" (13:1–2). "The cords of death encompassed me, and the torrents of ungodliness terrified me" (18:4).

David, who wrote many of the psalms, is described as the man after God's own heart (Acts 13:22). This is a lofty title, considering the outrageous sins David committed in his life, including adultery and murder. People often struggle with this paradox, but David isn't called a man after God's heart because he didn't sin or because God didn't take his sin seriously. David experienced severe consequences at the hand of God for his actions. I think David's unique relationship with God existed because, despite a few periods of silence, he did not cease to converse with God over the course of his life. The psalms show his intense struggle with fear of enemies and death, pain over his own sin and loss, and questioning when God would vindicate him. Through anger, depression, pain, loss, repentance, joy, exaltation, and worship, David expressed it all to God. God was his great Counselor, who both rebuked and honored him. When he sinned, David recognized it was against God. When he was afraid, he realized that God was the only one worthy of fear. When he suffered, David pleaded with God, knowing it was He alone who had the power to intervene. It was messy and ugly at times, but the conversation continued. Cain said nothing, but David said everything. Cain was cursed and David blessed.

David's example hit home with me several months ago. I had never thought of myself as an angry person. Depression I was familiar with, but anger was for loud, obnoxious people—not me. However, I began to notice that the smallest things would set me off in a fit of rage. Though I never actually destroyed anything, I had a strong desire to do so, and I was increasingly surprised at how volatile my emotions were. Where was this coming from? Surely this anger was not just about my computer not working as fast as I wanted or some car cutting me off on the road. So I began to ponder the questions, "Why am I angry? Why is my anger so close to the surface?"

I realized that I had been largely silent with God over a particular issue in my life. For many years I have desired to be married, yet God has not brought that about. Silence was my way of ignoring that pain, but it meant distance in my relationship with God. David was able to express his pain, bringing him wholeness; but this is easier said than done. Putting my anger into words was and is difficult because it makes me examine my anger. It becomes something tangible and something that must be dealt with rather than just an emotion that flares every so often. When God asks me why I am angry, part of me would rather clam up. Through prayer, meditation, and reading I have been better able to converse with God over difficult and sensitive issues. Breakthroughs came when I took seriously my belief in who God is as revealed in the Bible. I saw that my anger was an expression of my judgment on God and my disapproval of how He runs things. In judging God, my actions and emotions contradicted the very things I claimed to believe most dearly.

Jonah found himself in a similar situation. Of all things, Jonah was angry that God had chosen to spare the city of Nineveh when he, Jonah, did not think its people deserved to be spared. Jonah was so distraught and angry that he pleaded with God to take his life, "for death [was] better to [him] than life" (4:3). Then the Lord asked him, "Do you have good reason to be angry?" (4:4). It's interesting that God did not ask something like, "How dare you be angry?" or "Who are you to be angry with Me and speak to Me this way?" Jonah, unlike Cain, was willing to converse, despite his anger. And what a great question regarding anger! Jonah was angry over God's decision to have compassion rather than to destroy the pagan city. He stood in judgment against God, yet God was willing to continue His relationship with Jonah.

We condemn God, too, when we see someone whom we think is "less holy" than ourselves get something that we want. We become angry at God's apparent injustice. This is the feeling of the older son in the story of the prodigal son (see Luke 15:11–32). He is angry that his father throws a celebration for the son who has squandered the father's wealth. The older son reminds the father that he has always been faithful and hardworking but never had a party thrown in his honor. His anger is very similar to Jonah's and not far from Cain's. It is an anger based on selfishness, thinking that we know better than God as to what people deserve or should have. The problem is, of course, that if everyone got what they deserved, we would all find ourselves hopelessly lost.

As impossible as it might seem, there is such a thing as being angry and hitting the mark. Obviously, for the best example we have to look to Jesus. I already stated that our anger usually comes from the desire to protect our own honor. What about Jesus? The most common instance used to illustrate Jesus' anger is the "turning of the tables" or "cleansing of the temple." Matthew 21:12–13, Mark 11:15–18, and John 2:13–16 all give similar accounts of Jesus entering the temple courts and getting rid of the money changers and sellers. Jesus quotes from Isaiah 56:7 saying, "My house shall be called a house of prayer," and then He adds, "but you are making it a den of robbers." No doubt Jesus is angry, judging by His actions and words. But why? And how does He "hit the mark"? The answer might be a bit unexpected. Ironically, Jesus hits the mark with His anger for exactly the same reason that we miss it. He is angry because the people attempted to shame Him (though they did not know it), and He defends His own honor. The difference between Jesus and us is that Jesus has the right to do this. If God does not defend His own honor, who will? He will not yield His glory to anyone.

The phrase "righteous anger" or "righteous indignation" is often used with regard to Jesus' actions in this passage and others. For many people, though, this is too much of an oxymoron. The concept of righteous anger, however, is not a contradiction in spite of the misunderstandings. In Ezekiel 24:13b God speaks to the rebellious Israel saying, "You will not be *cleansed* from your filthiness again until I have spent My *wrath* on you." God's grace and mercy are sometimes wrapped in judgment. It is His wrath that will act as a catalyst, causing people to come to grips with their own weakness and inability.

Notice that the heading usually given to the Matthew 21 passage is "Jesus Cleanses the Temple." Somehow, with God, the emotion of anger and the action of cleansing go together. Anger is the impetus to cleansing. For us, so much of the time (as with Cain), anger is a pollutant and destroyer of our relationships because it is selfish and self-serving; but with God, anger is a purifier. It is a fire that devours unholiness and brings to the surface only that which reflects Him. God cannot react passively to sin because it is repulsive to Him and something He has to respond to. Our own offensiveness is mostly lost on us, as is God's righteous anger. We feel that others' violations against us are much more egregious than anything we have done against God. This sense of self-righteousness makes God's anger seem barbaric to us. But again, we don't see our sin clearly because we don't see God clearly.

This relationship between God and people is brought to life in C. S. Lewis's *Voyage of the Dawn Treader*. It tells the story of a spoiled little boy named Eustace, who finds himself and his two cousins magically transported to a ship sailing in another world. At one point in the journey, they come to a strange country, and Eustace wanders off and finds a cave filled with treasure. He lies down on the pile of treasure and puts on a golden bracelet before falling asleep. He awakens to discover that he has been changed into a dragon. Much to his dismay, Eustace cannot change himself back, so he remains a dragon for a while. Yet during that time, everyone notices that he behaves much better.

Finally, one night Eustace has an encounter with Aslan, the great lion. Aslan leads Eustace to a pool and instructs him to scratch the scales off his body. Try as he might, Eustace cannot get them all off. Aslan says he will have to do it. Using his claws, he begins to tear the scales away. Eustace describes the experience to his cousin:

> The very first tear he made was so deep that I thought it had gone right into my heart. And when he began pulling the skin off, it hurt worse than anything I've ever felt.[6]

Afterward he is healed and whole.

God's attempts to heal and purge us often feel painful, but they are necessary. Like Eustace, we in real life have a choice in how we respond to God's wrath and discipline. Remember that God is not surprised or thrown off by your anger or depression. The question is, will you learn and move through it?

Many times in the Scriptures God said He would delay His wrath that the people might be given the chance to repent, but "don't be deceived, God is not mocked; for whatever a man sows, this he will also reap" (Gal. 6:7). God's wrath and mercy are two extremes held in perfect balance. Just when you think His wrath is too harsh, you turn the pages of the Bible and find yourself wondering if His mercy is too lenient. He will judge the sinner when we would let it go, and He will forgive when we would demand the death penalty.

Not much is written on the wrath of God, but J. I. Packer wrote a chapter on the subject in his book *Knowing God*. Packer writes, "As a reaction to sin, God's wrath is an expression of his justice, and Paul [in Romans] rejects the suggestion 'that God is unjust to inflict wrath on us' (3:5 RSV)."[7] God would not be worthy if He did not have such a strong reaction to sin. His wrath does not detract from His perfection, but completes it.

There are other instances of this cleansing anger. The most striking example in the New Testament is in Galatians 2:11–14. In this passage, Paul recounts a situation with Peter. While the

Jews are not there in Jerusalem, Peter freely associates with the Gentiles, but as soon as the Jews arrive, Peter begins to distance himself and only associates with the Jews. Paul says, "I opposed him to his face, because he stood condemned" (2:11). Paul is not shy about expressing his disfavor with Peter's actions because he sees the dissension it created among the believers. Paul's anger acts as a purifying agent to rid the church of prejudice and favoritism. His anger is about defending the name of Christ and making sure that the church represents Him in truth. The early apostles also defended the gospel of Christ against heresy. They were not shy about making these false teachings and teachers known either in writing or in person. This was what Paul meant by hitting the mark with your anger.

To say that Cain failed to hit the mark seems like an understatement. He was angry and dejected because he was shamed by God's disfavor. He probably felt he deserved better and that his offering was just as good as Abel's. Cain's sin was not his anger but rather what he chose to do with that anger. When God asks you, as He asked Cain, "Why are you angry?" pay attention to what you should answer.

Conclusion and Reflection

When we are freed from the burden of defending our own sense of self, destructive anger dissipates. Do not forget God's warning to Cain in verse 7: "If you do well, will not your countenance be lifted up? And if you do not do well, sin is crouching at the door; and its desire is for you, but you must master it." Your self-serving anger will only lead to enslavement and destruction. We are instructed to be slow to anger (James 1:19), not because anger is wrong (note that it doesn't say never become angry), but because we must take the time to examine it and ourselves. Cleansing anger can only occur when we are more concerned with God's renown than our own.

- What triggers your anger most often?
- With whom are you angry? God? At another person?
- What do you hope to accomplish with your anger?
- To what do your angry words and actions lead?
- Are you thinking more about yourself or God when you are angry?
- How can your anger be used to edify and purify the church?
- How can your anger have other positive outcomes?

QUESTION #3

1 KINGS 19:9— "WHAT ARE YOU DOING HERE?"

> And the sweet season. Soon that joy was chased.
> And by new dread succeeded, when in view;
> A lion came, 'gainst me as it appear'd,
> With his head held aloft and hunger-mad,
> That e'en the air was fear-struck[8]
>
> —from *The Divine Comedy*

THIS QUESTION SEEMS to follow logically after giving an answer to the "Where are you?" question. Maybe you have had this conversation with a child:

Adult: Where are you?
Child: I'm over here.
Adult: Well, what are you doing here?

When the second question comes around, location is no longer the issue. "What are you doing here?" is asking for a reason. It could be rephrased, "Why are you here? Explain why you have come to this place."

Context

When God asks this question in 1 Kings 19:9, it is directed to Elijah the prophet. Elijah is first mentioned in 1 Kings 17, and his story continues on and off until he is taken by God into the heavens in 2 Kings 2. Throughout the New Testament and up to today, Elijah is regarded as one of the most important prophets in Israel's history. He appears along with Moses at the transfiguration of Christ in Matthew 7. Jesus calls Elijah one of His forerunners, similar to John the Baptist. Some people in the gospel accounts even think that Jesus is the resurrected Elijah (Matt. 16:14). Most interestingly, he is one of only two people who left this earth without dying; instead, he is taken up into the heavens by God in a chariot of fire (see Genesis 5:24 and 2 Kings 2:11). So how does a prophet as great as Elijah wind up huddled in the desert, asked by God, "What are you doing here?" It turns out the road from courageous to cowardly is not that far.

The context for this narrative begins in 1 Kings 18:18 and continues to 19:18. In 18:18–46 Elijah challenges Ahab, king of Israel, to gather all the pagan prophets (about 450) at Mount Carmel in order to see whose God/god is real. Ahab complies, and Elijah sets the rules. Baal's prophets and Elijah each set up an altar and prepare an ox for a burnt sacrifice. Each side then calls on their God/god to burn the animal, and the side that is answered will have the true God/god.

The prophets of Baal go first, and they weary themselves for many hours calling out to their god as Elijah taunts them mercilessly. Finally, it is Elijah's turn. But before calling on Yahweh, he pours several gallons of water over the altar and ox. When it is properly drenched, he prays aloud for the God of Israel to show His power. Immediately, fire flashes from heaven, devouring the sacrifice, water, and altar. The bystanders fall on their faces in worship, and Elijah commands them to slaughter the pagan prophets. As soon as they are all dead, Elijah tells Ahab to prepare for a rainstorm, which will break the drought (see 2 Kings 17). Elijah climbs to the top of the mountain to pray, and God answers by sending the rain clouds. By the power of God, Elijah then outruns Ahab's chariot all the way to the city of Jezreel (30 to 35 miles along the Kishon River).

By the end of 1 Kings 18, it seems easy to believe that Elijah was a foreshadowing of the Messiah. He is bold and uncompromising in every sense. This incident with the prophets of Baal is one of the most spectacular displays of courage and faith in the Scriptures. His faith waves like a banner as "the water flowed around the altar and he [Elijah] also filled the trench with water" (18:35). Elijah knows the fire of God can and will burn the altar; the water is for the sake of the people watching. Israel is an unfaithful bride, often wandering away to worship the pagan gods. Every so often they need reminding that the God of Israel is alive and well. Elijah knows this, as is evidenced in his prayer in 18:37: "Answer me, O Lord, answer me, that this people may know that You, O Lord, are God, and that You have turned their hearts back again." There's nothing like fire from heaven to turn people's hearts back to God.

So up to this point, Elijah has called down a drought on Israel, multiplied the widow's flour and oil to make bread, raised her son from the dead, challenged the pagan prophets, called down the rains to end the drought, and then ran about 30 miles to beat Ahab's chariot to Jezreel. Then comes 1 Kings 19.

Ahab tells his wife Jezebel all that Elijah has done, and she sends a threatening message to Elijah, saying she will have him killed by the next day. What follows in 1 Kings 19:3 is as troubling as it is puzzling: "And he [Elijah] was afraid and arose and ran for his life…" Yet somehow it's not so baffling; it's strangely familiar, like something you would like to forget but you can't. Part of me is glad that he was afraid and ran. It tells me that he was not so different from me. It tells me that sometimes, despite the evidence we see with our own eyes, we are still capable of acting irrationally.

Apparently, Elijah is in pretty good shape because he keeps running. He travels from Jezreel to Beersheba (about 90 miles), from Beersheba to the Sinai Desert, and finally to Mount Sinai for a total of just less than 400 miles in maybe three to four months. Though he wants to die along the way (19:4), the Lord sends an angel to provide food and water so that he can make it the rest of the way. God does not speak to Elijah until the end of this journey, after he reaches the mountain and finds a cave in which to stay. As with Jonah and Adam, God allows Elijah to run and hide, but He does not leave him alone.

"The voice of the Lord came to him [Elijah], and He said to him, 'What are you doing here, Elijah?'" Elijah answers honestly, describing how he has been doing God's work since there is no one else to do it and how now people are trying to kill him, too. His answer is similar to Adam's: "I was afraid so I ran and hid myself." In contrast, Elijah isn't afraid of God; he is afraid of Queen Jezebel, who threatened to kill him. Adam and Jonah try to hide from God (for different reasons), but Elijah hides on Mount Sinai—the Mountain of God. It's as though by going to God, the source, he is trying to get back something he has lost.

Digging Deeper

With the possible exception of Moses, few had experienced the miraculous power of God like Elijah had. We are tempted to look on the ancients and scold them for their disbelief so quickly after God performed a miracle. How could you doubt or turn away after such evidence? How could Elijah have been afraid of a pagan woman's threat to his life after he had just defeated 450 of Baal's prophets? This is the tension every believer in God faces, no matter the circumstances: the desire to believe versus the tendency to disbelieve.

To be fair, we must ask, "Is it even rational to believe in God?" There isn't room here to delineate the arguments for the existence of God developed over the centuries and debated still today. However, I do encourage you to read the thoughtful books written on this topic. For our purposes here, as I stated in the introduction, we will assume the truth and authenticity of the Bible (there are sound justifications for assuming this). With this foundation, then, is it rational to believe in God? When Elijah felt afraid for his life and ran, was he being rational or irrational? Did it make sense or did it not make sense, given the situation? Was his fear justified? Yes… and no.

Elijah's lapse of trust in God is something we understand, not because it was rational, but because we are all, at times, irrational beings. Our choices always seem logical at the time, as though they were something that had to be done. I'm sure Elijah felt there was nothing else he could have done. Jezebel was certainly not a queen to take lightly. She had already killed and persecuted other prophets of God. Why would Elijah be spared when others hadn't been? How can we be expected to trust God in such situations?

This question of trust and reason came up several years ago during a leadership retreat I attended in the mountains. Among the various challenges that were along an obstacle course, one that we did was called the "Leap of Faith." Each person had to climb a ladder up a tree to a small wooden platform about thirty feet high. The goal was to leap off the platform and grab a bar hanging about eye level, but four feet away. Before you think we were completely crazy, I should mention that we had support ropes and spotters. I remember so vividly one of the guys yelling out as he stood on the platform, "This is so unnatural!" When it was finally my turn, I wholeheartedly agreed. Everything in me said it was a bad idea to jump off that platform and that the chances of my grabbing the bar were slim to none. I was shaking even with the ropes tied securely and with the spotters below.

The entire concept of faith and trust suddenly made sense to me. The strange thing was that if you had asked me at any point whether I was afraid of bodily harm, I would have said "no." My reason told me that these people would not be in business if they regularly (or ever) dropped someone. I also had watched several people go before me, and not one of them was injured, though they were a little shaky. I had every reason not to be afraid, yet I was. Why? Because I was not in the habit of jumping off platforms in an attempt to grab a bar. It was unnatural in that sense, and so is faith. According to the Bible, disbelief is natural, whereas faith is supernatural. Faith challenges my natural inclination to trust only what is comfortable, pleasant, and familiar to me. Faith, however, does not replace what we experience with our senses; faith must go above and beyond the senses. The phrase "Leap of Faith" is actually misleading because it implies that there is no context for our faith, as though God asks us to jump without giving us something to stand on. Just as I had a good context for believing in my physical safety standing and jumping off that platform, God has given us a context to our faith, not only in our own lives but also through the lives of the patriarchs. Only through spiritual eyes does belief in God make any sense.

Shortly after this experience in acrobatics, I came across Hebrews 11:17 and 19 in the middle of the famous "heroes of faith" chapter. Verses 17 and 19 read, "By faith Abraham, when he was tested, offered up Isaac, and he who had received the promises was offering up his only begotten son... He [Abraham] considered (or reasoned) that God is able to raise people even from the dead." Abraham thought back on his experiences with God and how He had kept His promises all along the way. God did not ask Abraham to sacrifice his son on their first encounter, but only after more than twenty-five years of walking together did God ask such a thing. Then Abraham *reasoned* that the God who had called him to be a nation would not leave him childless. He considered and weighed all he knew about God, what God had said to him, and the things God had done. Abraham rightly and rationally concluded that God could probably raise people from the dead (though he had not seen it), and perhaps that was exactly what He would do for Isaac. The point is that Abraham was rational to place his faith in God and sacrifice his only son, despite what it may seem or how it felt. Elijah was irrational to run away and to disbelieve God's power to protect him, despite what it may have seemed or how it felt.

There are many today who would criticize the idea of faith, saying that it is belief in something that cannot be seen or for which there is no evidence. They claim that faith is an attempt to deny the obvious reality that we are alone in the universe and there is no real purpose to life. The so-called "rationalists" claim to assume or know only what they can see and touch or otherwise verify through scientific inquiry. Ironically, those who would define their reality in such a narrow way are often the ones who call Christians "narrow-minded." What they don't see is that faith does not *narrow* one's view; rather, faith must *broaden* it. Faith is not blind, and it is not an effort to muster up belief in something or someone that isn't there. God does not ask us to bumble around in the dark. Faith is what helps us to see the truth that exists beyond our senses, beyond the here and now. "Now faith is the *assurance* of things hoped for, the *conviction* of things not seen" (Heb. 11:1). Through faith we can be assured and convinced of those things for which we have hope. If we are honest about it, even the most skeptical of skeptics has faith in certain things: his or her own existence, that the next moment will arrive, the existence of others and the world around them, the reality of the past, and so on. Some things must be certain, or we can know nothing at all.

Faith according to Christianity, though, must include a willingness to examine all evidence. This means not excluding some fact just because it suits me or makes me uncomfortable. We are not afforded this luxury in which the world partakes. Faith and reason have been pitted against each other for so long that we don't see there is no reason without faith and no faith without reason.

God was justified in asking Elijah, "What are you doing here?" God had shown Himself in many dramatic ways, yet Elijah still ran for his life. However, God did not seem angry or even critical. In fact, God provided for him along the way, and this fact should encourage us. When we run or wander, God is often at our heels. At the same time, like Elijah, we find that wherever we go God has arrived there first and has been waiting for us.

What is unique here about Elijah (as opposed to Jonah or Adam) is his choice of refuge. Elijah did not hide from God, as I pointed out earlier; rather, he ran to God. Elijah went to Mount Sinai, also called the Mountain of God. This was where Moses talked with God face-to-face and received the original Ten Commandments (see Exodus 19–20). It was where God made His presence evident to the people of Israel. Elijah could not have gone there to hide from God. As a warrior weary from battle, Elijah climbed the mountain to meet with God. His natural instinct had been to run in the face of fear, to disbelieve God's power to protect him.

In *The Divine Comedy*, Dante portrays himself as taking a similar, though symbolic, journey. In the first canto, Dante climbs a mountain and is assailed by wild animals:

> And the sweet season. Soon that joy was chased.
> And by new dread succeeded, when in view
> A lion came, 'gainst me as it appear'd,
> With his head held aloft and hunger-mad,
> That e'en the air was fear-struck.[9]

One commentator writes, "The poem is the narrative of a journey down through Hell, up the mountain of Purgatory, and through the revolving heavens into the presence of God."[10] This description seems analogous to Elijah's journey with God, as well as to yours and mine. Our journey with and towards God involves a bit of everything from fear to everlasting joy.

Not long after running from Jezebel, Elijah went to Mount Sinai, believing he would see God. I wonder what he expected, though. Did Elijah think God would sing his praises for being a good prophet? Did he expect God to console him or give sympathy? Did he anticipate God's question? I don't know what Elijah expected from God, but I do think that he expected God to be there. When we mess up and allow fear to win over faith, our tendency can be to run where we think God can't see us, or at the least we ignore Him. Elijah didn't do this. He went to where he knew God would be.

But Elijah wasn't to stay there forever, evidenced by God's question to him. God's questions are always intended to spark action or change of some kind. The question "What are you doing here?" suggests that there is somewhere else to be. Elijah went looking for God, but God had been with him all along. When Elijah had given his reason for why he was there, God instructed him, "Go forth and stand on the mountain before the Lord" (1 Kings 19:11). There was a great wind, an earthquake, and a fire.

It is interesting to note that a similar description of the Lord's presence on Mount Sinai can be found in Exodus 19:18, when God gave Moses the Ten Commandments. "Now Mount Sinai was all in smoke because the Lord descended upon it in fire; and its smoke ascended like the smoke of a furnace, and the whole mountain quaked violently." The people were terrified, and Moses explained, "Do not be afraid; for God has come in order to test you, and in order that the fear of Him may remain with you, so that you may not sin" (Ex. 20:20).

This time, however, God was not in any of these elements. When Elijah heard the sound of a gentle breeze, he wrapped his face and stood at the entrance of the cave to speak with the Lord. Elijah knew the Lord well enough to recognize what He sounded like. Then the strangest thing happened. The Lord repeated His question, and Elijah repeated his answer, word for word. I have to think that God was looking for something more in Elijah's answer the second time around. I know that when I repeat a question to my students, it is usually because they did not give me the answer I wanted the first time or they didn't understand the question. A word to the wise: after God asks you twice, "What are you doing here?" repent and find out where you should be.

God didn't wait for Elijah to ask where he should be, He just told him. Essentially, God told Elijah to go back the way he had come and to anoint two future kings and the prophet Elisha, who would take his place. Here's a rough and condensed translation of the entire conversation:

Elijah: I want to die.
God: What are you doing here, Elijah?
Elijah: I was afraid because they are trying to kill me like they killed all your other prophets.
God: What are you doing here, Elijah?
Elijah: I was afraid because they are trying to kill me like they killed all your other prophets.
God: Go back the way you came and anoint Jehu and Hazael to be kings and Elisha as the prophet to take your place. Don't worry; I will protect you.

There are two things here. First, God allowed Elijah to have his time on the mountain. God could have intervened or prevented him from going. God understands our weaknesses and our tendency to run away, but He will always call us back like He did with Elijah. Second, God was not going to allow Elijah to stay there (and he probably would have stayed). God does not leave His people to their own devices or to find their own way.

God gives gifts and tasks to each of us. When He asks you, "What are you doing here?" it's a nudge to get going in the direction in which He is calling you. It is an indication you have been led away from the path. Faith or belief in God is what must guide our steps; any steps we take that are not in faith will ultimately lead us to sin (Rom. 14:23; 2 Cor. 5:7; Gal. 5:5–6).

Conclusion and Reflection

Elijah was a great man of God who still found it difficult to remain faithful. We should not be surprised, then, when we find ourselves wandering off the narrow road God has marked for us. Any true disciple will have to answer this question at some point: What are you doing here?

- When you stray from the Lord, what reasons do you use to explain your actions?
- Are your reasons rational or irrational? Explain.
- Do your reasons for wandering away make sense, knowing that God is wise, good, and powerful?
- What role does faith play in your Christian life?
- What context has God given you for your faith?
- Have you ever had to believe something "blindly," that is, believe that something was true without any context or background?
- What do you know of God from your own experience, and what do you believe by faith?

QUESTION #4

JOB 38:1-2— "WHO IS THIS THAT DARKENS COUNSEL BY WORDS WITHOUT KNOWLEDGE?"

"Rat!" he found breath to whisper, shaking. "Are you afraid?"

"Afraid?" murmured the Rat, his eyes shining with unutterable love. "Afraid! Of *Him*? O, never, never! And yet—and yet—O, Mole, I am afraid!"[11]

—from *The Wind in the Willow*

THE EXISTENCE OF pain, suffering, and evil grips everyone at some time or another. Some people seem to get a double portion, whereas others get by with a few scratches. Job was one of those people who received a double, maybe even a triple, portion. He is best known for the suffering and heartache he endured and his struggle with God through his terrible ordeal. The account of Job is rich and deep in meaning, as it tackles some of the most difficult questions and provides some of the most unexpected answers.

Context

The book of Job is unique in some ways. Because there is never any mention of Israel or the Mosaic Law, it is probable that Job lived prior to Moses and Abraham. This puts him between Genesis 4 and 11, though there is no mention of him in those chapters. It is not stated who wrote the book, but Job himself is the most likely candidate. Also, the style of Job stands in contrast to most of the other books in the Bible. With the exception of chapters 1–2 and a brief portion in the end, the book of Job is written as poetry. In general, each chapter presents one of Job's three friends stating his point of view on Job's suffering. Job also shares his anguish and cries out to God, and then God speaks in the final chapters.

The first two chapters set the stage for the rest of the book. We are told that Job is "blameless, upright, fearing God, and turning away from evil" (Job 1:1). He is also wealthy and has ten children. Then the scene turns to the throne room of heaven. Satan enters, and God asks him what he'd been doing. He responds, "I've been wandering around." God asks him if he has considered Job, the God-fearing man. Satan replies, "Does Job fear God for nothing?" (1:9). The accuser points out that Job's faith has never been properly tested so he has no reason *not* to fear the Lord. So God gives Satan permission to test Job, and within a short period of time, his children are dead, his wealth is gone, and he falls horribly ill with painful boils all over his body.

After all this, Job's wife tells him, "Curse God and die!" (2:9). Then verse 10 demonstrates the true character of Job: "'Shall we indeed accept good from God and not accept adversity?' In all this Job did not sin with his lips." Job's statement to his wife demonstrates tremendous insight into the character of God. We are so prone, as a fallen people, to believe that if we do good things we will be rewarded with a comfortable life. We tend to think the bad circumstances in our lives should be alleviated by the good things we do. Isaiah 45:7 is perhaps not the most popular verse in the Bible: "The One forming the light and creating darkness, causing well-being and creating calamity; I am the Lord who does all these." And Matthew 5:45b is part of Jesus' Sermon on the Mount: "For

JOB 38:1–2— "WHO IS THIS THAT DARKENS COUNSEL BY WORDS WITHOUT KNOWLEDGE?"

He causes His sun to rise on the evil and the good, and sends rain on the righteous and the unrighteous."

Then Job's three friends come to visit. "When they lifted up their eyes at a distance and did not recognize him, they raised their voices and wept.... Then they sat down on the ground with him for seven days and seven nights with no one speaking a word to him, for they saw that his pain was very great" (2:12–13). Just in case we are tempted to make light of Job's suffering, this account alone makes Job's anguish clear. His pain is so great that his friends are speechless…but only at first.

The friends would have done well to mourn and sympathize with Job and then return home. However, like many friends, they think it necessary to make their opinions known. They are convinced that God only reserves this kind of treatment for those who have committed a serious sin. The men urge Job to confess whatever secret sin he is hiding and be done with it, but Job stands by his record: "Teach me, and I will be silent; and show me how I have erred…. Now please look at me, and see if I lie to your face" (6:24, 28). Later, Job gets a little more upset with his so-called friends: "Truly then you are the people, and with you wisdom will die! But I have intelligence as well as you; I am not inferior to you" (12:2–3).

Job insists he has not done anything to deserve what has happened to him, but at the same time, he claims God's righteousness. One of his most poignant statements is in 13:15: "Though He slay me, I will hope in Him. Nevertheless, I will argue my ways before Him." Job recognizes that even though it is God who is bringing about his suffering, God is also his only hope; but Job does not plan to suffer quietly. These are tremendous truths that Job is holding in tension: 1) God is allowing my suffering and not alleviating it. 2) God is my only hope of relief from suffering. And finally, 3) I can and I will let Him know how upset I am about this suffering. As the chapters roll on, Job demands an answer from the Lord; he demands to have the chance to make his case known to the God who would slay a righteous man. Though the friends rebuke Job for being prideful, he is not swayed.

Interestingly, God is silent through all this rhetoric, until chapter 38. Finally God speaks, but He only addresses Job, blatantly leaving out the three friends. Contrary to how He appears to Elijah, God speaks to Job out of the whirlwind (38:1). This just proves God doesn't always speak in the same way. Different people and different situations call for different tactics.

After listening to Job, God asks His first of a series of questions: "Who is this that darkens counsel by words without knowledge?" The New Living Translation puts it this way: "Who is this that questions my wisdom with such ignorant words?" God proceeds to ask Job a litany of rhetorical questions about whether or not he controls the wind, snow, hail, sun, moon, day, night, seasons, light, darkness, and stars. God asks if Job is aware of the various animals and their needs in the wild. It isn't just Job's knowledge that God was questioning; it is his authority and power over the universe. God says to Job, if you can do all these things, "then I will also confess to you, that your own right hand can save you" (40:14). In other words, if Job is equal with God, he won't need God's salvation because Job can save himself. There are over fifty questions in chapters 38–41, and Job cannot answer "yes" to a single one.

Digging Deeper

God's line of questioning here is at first a little puzzling. Our instincts might be to think, "But this doesn't really answer Job's question about his suffering!" And it would seem so. We sympathize with Job's suffering and his demand for an answer because many of us have been in that same boat. God's way of answering Job is unexpected, and some would venture to say, unsatisfying and unfair. However, understanding God's answer here is critical, for it centers on one of the most difficult problems facing Christianity. We must assume that God has given the best possible answer, and it is our thinking that must be adjusted.

The problem of evil in the world is perhaps the most compelling argument against the existence of the Christian God. Those grappling with Christianity are the ones who have the most trouble juxtaposing belief in God with the existence of evil. Most other religions, as well as the atheist worldview, must accept evil because they believe God is impersonal, indifferent, incapacitated, or simply nonexistent. Some religions would even have us believe that evil does not exist at all. Based on these worldviews, evil must be tolerated or ignored. Yet this does not seem satisfactory, especially for the person suffering.

Anyone attempting to deal with the problem of evil in this world must be willing to take evil seriously. A worldview that denies or belittles evil is not dealing with reality. The Hindu religion goes so far as to blame the person suffering. The rule of karma is that a person suffers due to sins committed in a previous life, so the suffering is deserved and must not be alleviated. If the atheist remains consistent with his or her worldview, then the best answer he or she can give to someone suffering from evil is, "It doesn't really matter." The Christian Scientist would simply say that the Holocaust never really happened because the material world does not really exist. These logical conclusions from these worldviews and religions are highly unsatisfactory, incongruent with reality, and even despairing. They offer little to no hope or justice to the one suffering from evil.

However, Christianity claims that God is personal, just, compassionate, and omnipotent. But if God is all these things, how could something like the Holocaust have happened—an evil so profound and so dark that its shadow still hovers over us? Thus, the complaint against the coexistence of God and evil is largely a complaint against the *Christian* God. The Christian worldview stands accused of being internally inconsistent, and if the accusation is found true, then Christians must abandon ship to seek a better way. Since biblical Christianity is what makes us aware of this seemingly incongruent reality, it makes sense to search for a solution within the Christian worldview, as portrayed in the Bible, to see if one is offered.

It was Alvin Plantinga, a noted philosopher, who articulated a possible way to bridge these two apparently contradictory truths within the Christian worldview—that is, the coexistence of God and evil. Plantinga postulates what is called the "Free Will Defense."[12] It states that God, being a morally free being, created humans with similar moral freedom to act and will as they choose. We are free to choose those actions that benefit, or harm, others and ourselves. If the individual is truly free, then no one or nothing is directly responsible for actions taken except that individual. While God is sovereign and omnipotent, He does not predetermine or control people's actions. To be truly free to choose good, one must also have the option of choosing evil.

Some might argue that people do not have free will but are compelled by social and biological conditioning to behave in certain ways. However, the logical conclusion of this reasoning is horrific. If we accept that people are *not* free, we deny their responsibility; and to deny personal responsibility means that we can no longer justly punish individuals for crimes they have committed. On this argument, the soldiers of Nazi Germany should not have been punished for killing millions of people since they were not free to make that choice. No one would want to live in a world where this view was accepted and carried out. Therefore, it seems necessary that people are free to make moral choices and that they are held accountable for them. A just society depends on it.

The impact of Plantinga's argument is significant in that it shows how the existence of God and the existence of evil are not necessarily a logical contradiction. The Christian worldview takes into account all three truths necessary for this conclusion: the existence of a just and loving God, the existence of evil, and the free will of humankind to choose moral actions (both good and evil in the objective sense). Therefore, belief in the Christian God is not illogical or inconsistent based on the evidence of evil in the world. While this belief answers the logical problem of evil (which is an important step), it may still fail to comfort someone who is suffering.

Job would have agreed with Plantiga's argument. He believed God to be just and merciful and was at first willing to accept the good and the bad from God, but how was Job to interpret the intensity and duration of his suffering? If God is indeed just and merciful, why was this happening? The logical problem of evil and suffering became much more personal. This is where many of us relate. We are torn and conflicted on a deeply emotional, rather than a philosophical, level.

Perhaps the most difficult part to understand is when God gives Satan permission to attack Job. The only thing more frightening would be if Satan didn't have to ask permission. But why would God do this? God did not allow Satan to test Job because he had sinned in some way and had to be punished. It wasn't a punishment at all, though it surely felt that way. God's purpose was to bring Job into a deeper and more meaningful relationship with Him. Job understood God at a certain level, and all was right in his corner of the world. Job offered sacrifices for sins committed by his family. He was generous, righteous, honest, and God-fearing. The Bible even goes so far as to say that Job was "the greatest of all the men of the east" (1:3b).

Then God changed the rules, seemingly. Though Job knew that God was in control, he didn't understand why God allowed the suffering to come into his life. In his mind, he did not deserve to have these things happen. He had served God and remained blameless, but God is less concerned with our creaturely comforts than we would like to believe. God is willing to have us suffer when He knows that in the end we will know Him better and more deeply. Note that God does not allow pain for suffering's sake; with God, there is always purpose and design. In God's economy, nothing is wasted.

So God answered Job's questions with a question of His own: "Who is this that darkens counsel by words without knowledge?" This is like a thundercloud speaking to an ant, and somehow the ant survives. God's questions in these chapters are designed to teach two things: God is God, and Job is not. Humility is the lesson to be learned. Micah 6:8 states, "What does the Lord require of you? To do justice, to love kindness and to walk humbly with your God." What strikes me about this verse is the last part, "…walk humbly with your God." So many other words could have been put in the place of "humbly," but it is there for the very reason that there is no other way to walk with Him. No one can walk with the Lord in the self-deception called pride. To walk with the Lord is to be in awe, fear, and reverence; it is to recognize our creaturely status in the universe.

In Isaiah 45:11–12 God asks, "Do you question what I do? Do you give Me orders about the work of My hands? I am the one who made the earth and created people to live in it. With My hands I stretched out the heavens. All the millions of stars are at My command." God created, and so God commands. Our relationship with the Almighty God extends as far as our willingness to live and walk in humility. We have to come to the point of realizing that our humility before God is essential to our relationship with Him. When we are humble, we become great (Prov. 11:2; Prov. 29:23; 1 Peter 5:6) because we have understood our place; we have understood what is real and true.

There is a great illustration of humility, awe, and love in a scene from *The Wind in the Willows*. Rat and Mole are rowing down a river when they hear the sound of a flute being played. They are mystified by this and wonder who could be playing it. Suddenly, the musician is revealed to be a faun, a creature of such grace and dignity that Rat and Mole are stupefied...

> "Rat!" he found breath to whisper, shaking. "Are you afraid?"
> "Afraid?" murmured the Rat, his eyes shining with unutterable love. "Afraid! Of *Him*? O, never, never! And yet—and yet—O, Mole, I am afraid!"[13]

This must be how we approach God—with unutterable love and fear.

Much of the teaching on the relationship between God and people centers on the "warm and fuzzy." Jesus is our buddy through difficult times. He's there to give us a hug and wipe away tears. He carries us, consoles us, pats us on the back, and says that everything is going to work out for the good. There is nothing inherently wrong with these beliefs; rather, the problem is that they are imbalanced. Certainly Jesus is our friend in times of need (and otherwise), but He is also the Lord and Maker of the universe. The God who wept over the death of His friend Lazarus (John 11:35) also reigns in fearsome glory in the throne room of heaven (Is. 6:1–7).

In his outstanding book *Reaching for the Invisible God*, Philip Yancey describes a personal experience of visiting a Russian Orthodox church. The Western Christians were criticizing the orthodox rituals, claiming that they make God seem far away and inapproachable, but Yancey notes that there is some truth in the ritual. The Russian Orthodox priest demonstrates with his candles, stole, incense, and crucifix "that you do not approach the Other as you would approach your own kind... If you find God with great ease...perhaps it is not God that you have found."[14] God is on our side, and He has loved us with unspeakable love, but He is not to be taken lightly nor approached casually.

Humility is essential to the Christian life because it is the foundation of our relationship with God. If pride is the root of sin and humility is the opposite of pride, then humility is the root of righteousness or right living. If pride is the lie and the destruction of my relationships with God and others, then humility is the truth and the restoration of my relationships.

In chapter 1, the discussion was on Genesis 3 and the fall. The first verses of that chapter become relevant again here because of how the serpent tempted Eve. He convinced her that she would become "like God" in knowing all things and implied that God was keeping something good from her. Eve's pride (and ours) believed this and fell out of fellowship with God. When we believe this prideful attitude to be an accurate worldview, we are distanced from God because we are not seeing Truth.

Humility is a core attitude, a mind-set, a way of thinking, and a way of behaving—it is a worldview. Humility towards God states, "You alone are God, the Creator. I must serve and worship You, not for any other reason than that You are worthy." The one who is humble acknowledges that only God is great, and he or she is not resentful of this fact but is relieved and even joyful for it.

Many of us are accustomed to thinking that God is worthy of our worship and service only because of the things He has done for us. This is not the case! Even if God had done nothing to save us from our own choice of rebellion, He would still be worthy, simply because He is God. The fact that He is who He is remains reason enough for us—His creation—to live and walk in humility. How much more, then, and how much better to consider all that He has done for us! Instead of motivating us only out of fear, He has loved us first that we might return His love. Miracle of miracles, it is His desire to relate to us, and in His relating to us, we are recreated.

What is God's answer to Job's suffering and your suffering? What is God's answer to the problem of evil invading our lives? His answer to Job is the same as it is for us. "Look around you. Look at this world and everything in it. If I can hold the sun in its place, if I can command the rain and wind, if I can oversee the beasts, then surely I am capable of handling your life." In my moments of doubt, it is the evidence of creation that assures me time and again of God's existence, care, and power. There are stars in our galaxy that dwarf the size of the sun. If our solar system was the size of a quarter, then the Milky Way Galaxy would be the size of North America. And this is only one galaxy amidst a universe of countless galaxies! God has made them all and named each star one by one (Is. 40:26). None of it escapes His attention. This is the kind of God whom we can trust with our lives.

God invited Job to examine His handiwork, to evaluate the various things He had accomplished. He did not try to explain to Job the problem of evil and suffering because it is much too complicated. I once heard someone comment that for God to explain the problem of evil to us would be like Einstein trying to explain the theory of relativity to a clam. Some things are beyond us and always will be, and some things will be revealed later.

However, God's answer to our most difficult questions is simply Himself. Our answer is not in a book or in philosophical arguments, but it is in a person; it is in the very nature and character of God. To find joy and satisfaction in this answer is to know peace. Ultimately, the answer to our most desperate need is found in the person of Jesus. The book of 2 Corinthians is a great testament to this fact. Paul writes, "Indeed, we had the sentence of death within ourselves so that we would not trust in ourselves, but in God who raises the dead" (1:9). Paul explains that the purpose behind much of our suffering and struggle is *so that we will not trust in ourselves*. It's as though God is wrestling with us to gain our attention. Since we can't trust in ourselves, Paul said that we trust in the God who raises the dead. Why? Because the God who can raise the dead must be the One who is in control. If He can raise the dead, what can He not do? There is nothing out of His reach, so our trust must be in

Him. Jesus (because of the resurrection) is the evidence on which we base our trust.

How did Job respond to God's questions? He did not respond with complaints, arguments, anger, or depression, because these had all been done (go back to the previous chapters). Job's answer to God's questions was acknowledgment of what was true:

> I know that You can do all things [even raise the dead], and that no purpose of Yours can be thwarted [even allowing suffering into my life].... I have heard of You by the hearing of the ear; But now my eye sees You; Therefore I retract and I repent in dust and ashes.
>
> —Job 42:2, 5–6

In *The Case for Faith*, Lee Strobel interviews Peter Kreeft, a Christian philosopher, professor, and author. Strobel is confronting Kreeft with the problem of evil and the existence of God. Naturally, the conversation turns to Job. Kreeft responds:

> [God] says to Job, "Who are you? Are you God? Did you write this script? Were you there when I laid the foundations of the earth?" And Job realizes the answer is no. Then he is satisfied. Why? Because he sees God!...I think Job gets a foretaste of heaven at the end of the book of Job, because he meets God...As we look at human relationships, what we see is that lovers don't want explanations, but presence. And what God is, essentially, is presence.[15]

God wants a relationship with us for the same reason that He established the covenant with ancient Israel: "To be God to you and to your descendants after you" (Gen. 17:7b). God will not be manipulated in any way; rather, He will decide the terms, and we must live by them.

Conclusion and Reflection

Job learned that God does not fit in a box or follow "rules" that we have made for Him. God, like C. S. Lewis's great lion, Aslan, will not be tamed, but we can (we must) trust in His goodness. Trust is all that matters in our relationship with God; if He couldn't be entrusted with our lives and to do what is best for us, then we would be truly lost.

- What has God taught you in and through past difficulties?
- What is He teaching you now?
- What answer to your suffering would satisfy you?
- How is humility a part of your relationship with God, especially through difficult times?

QUESTION #5

MATTHEW 9:28— "DO YOU BELIEVE I AM ABLE TO DO THIS?"

> It is we Christians who accept all actual evidence—it is you rationalists who refuse actual evidence being constrained to do so by your creed. But I am not constrained by any creed in the matter, and looking impartially into the miracles of medieval and modern times, I have come to the conclusion that they occurred.[16]
>
> —from *Orthodoxy*

THE GOSPEL WRITERS, and even historical writers outside of Christianity, portray Jesus as a miracle worker. Matthew 9 is no exception. In this chapter alone, Jesus healed a paralytic, raised a girl from the dead, stopped a woman's hemorrhaging, healed two blind men, and cast out a demon. These kinds of accounts immediately raise questions as well as eyebrows. The question "Do you believe I am able to do this?" becomes that much more relevant in our age and culture of disbelief.

Context

The context for this next question involves three dramatic healing miracles done by Jesus. Matthew 9:18–26 is the account of Jesus raising a little girl from the dead. She had been very ill, and her father approaches Jesus, asking Him to come to the house and heal her. As he is asking this, a messenger comes and tells the father that the girl has died. On His way to the house, a woman suffering from a bleeding disorder touches Jesus' clothes, and she is healed. Jesus offers her these words in verse 22: "Daughter, take courage; your faith has made you well." When He arrives at the girl's house, Jesus says she is only sleeping and raises her up. Verse 26 tells us that "…this news spread throughout all that land."

Following these events, Jesus goes on and two blind men start calling out to Him, "Have mercy on us, Son of David!" Apparently Jesus does not want to converse with them in the open because He waits until He is inside a house before responding to their plea. That the men use the term "Son of David" shows they view Jesus as being the Messiah, though it is likely they do not know all of what that means. Jesus turns to them and asks, "Do you believe I am able to do this?"

Digging Deeper

In recent conversations with non-Christians, I have encountered not only unbelief in the Bible, but also hostility and scorn. As is expected in our Western culture—which is epistemologically confined to science and the scientific method—the major hang-up for most people is the miracle accounts. Many people claim that those events just couldn't have happened; they're too far-fetched and unscientific. Looking at some of the stories in the Bible, it's understandable that someone might find them bizarre and unlikely. There are the ten plagues of Egypt, a talking donkey, people raised from the dead, a floating ax head, a virgin birth, angels, demons, fire, smoke, and the list continues. If you have never heard one of these stories (and even if you have), many of them sound fit for children's books, fairy tales, or even science fiction.

However, the problem does not lie within the history itself. The problem comes in how we answer one simple question: What do I believe about God? If there is no God, of course these stories are unlikely, for who can alter the laws of nature? For the atheist there is no God outside of the universe, and for many people the universe itself becomes god. If this is the case, miracles such as those described in the Bible would be unthinkable because we cannot expect an impersonal universe to suddenly change its own rules. Furthermore, if there is no God, can we even call them "rules" or "laws"? If all of life evolved as some random sequence of events, how can we even make predictions, speculations, or hypotheses concerning the natural world? With no mind to create or govern it, we should not expect to have accurate observations about a random universe.

The fact is that we *can* make accurate observations about the universe because we find that it is not completely random. There are events that tend to follow other events and causes that lead to certain effects. In physics, we learn that time is the element in our universe that keeps things from happening all at once. It gives us progression and cause and effect. These constructs are so much a part of our human experience that it is very difficult to discuss them objectively as some distant observer.

If I told you a person walked a mile in sixty seconds, you would think it was a joke, because time doesn't allow for such an event. But what if someone came along and did walk a mile in sixty seconds? It couldn't happen; you would say it's not even possible. This is the reaction of many people to Jesus' miracles, both back then and today. In many of His miracles, Jesus was essentially manipulating time in such a way that the real miracle wasn't the event itself but the immediacy of it. Similarly, walking a mile isn't so special, but doing it in sixty seconds would be impressive.

One of the best examples of this is Jesus' first miracle, recorded in John 2, which takes place in Cana. Jesus takes some large containers of water and turns them instantaneously into wine. In reality, water into wine is not so far fetched; it is a well-established process in nature. Yet when this process is left on its own, it takes several months. Jesus accomplished this task in a moment. First Peter 3:8 states very plainly, "With the Lord a day is like a thousand years and a thousand years is like a day."

Perhaps the most memorable miracles are the people Jesus raised from the dead. I had previously thought of these as healing miracles, which is not inaccurate, only incomplete. In raising a person from the dead Jesus was manipulating time. We are so accustomed to a "forward" motion of time that for time to move backward is nearly unthinkable. Again, in physics the second law of thermodynamics tells us that the universe is in a state of entropy. This means that the universe and its systems are always moving toward a state of increased chaos and decomposition. Jesus defied this law by reversing, at least temporarily, the deadly effects of entropy. The little girl rose from her bed, and Lazarus walked out of the tomb.

The devastating and fatal effects of time and entropy are results of sin. When Jesus demonstrated His power to reverse these effects, He was demonstrating not only power over the laws of the universe, but also His power over the consequences of sin. Of course, His ultimate victory was on the cross. In heaven, the constraints and pains of time, chaos, and decay will be removed. These arrows will be reversed, as it were. Our experience in eternity will be that of ever-increasing wholeness, completion, and joy.

The concept and acceptance of miracles can be difficult when we fail to recognize that many events happening around us every day are, in fact, miraculous. Every birth is a miracle, largely unexplainable by science. We find water into wine unthinkable, yet we accept seeds into grapevine. The very fact that life exists on this planet is incredibly improbable. Scientists used to think that gravity could have been a little stronger or weaker and everything would still have turned out the same. They know now that if things like gravity or the mass of a proton had been altered the tiniest fraction, human existence would not have been possible anywhere in our universe. These are all miracles, but we are desensitized and unimpressed because these things are a part of our common human experience.

In chapter 8, Matthew records the incident of Jesus calming the great storm. The disciples respond in disbelief. "Who is He?" they ask. We, like the disciples, have a list of things that are OK and things that are not. It's OK for a storm to rise but not for someone to command it to stop and it to do so. It's OK for someone to get sick and die but not to be raised from the dead. It's OK for it to rain but not for a flood so massive that nothing survives except a family who builds a boat. When we think this way, God becomes small in our eyes.

For Christians, our worldview must include the God of the Bible. As the saying goes, we were made in the image of God, not God in the image of man. It was He who created the physical and natural laws that we cling to so dearly and think we explain so well. We think we can define reality by our small understanding of these laws and how they operate. A cursory reading of Job 38–42 should change that notion.

Breaches in these laws are not so unthinkable when you see that it is only God operating within laws that we have not begun to understand and possibly never will. We cannot claim to know God fully, so how can we know all of what He has made? He is not inhibited by the same laws as we are. It is difficult to imagine a being not limited by time, space, gravity, and so on, but what kind of God is trapped by what He created?

When we encounter those in the world who would challenge the reality of these biblical miracles, we must remind them of the miracles they witness every day. There is hardly a better explanation for these than for those miracles that are rarer. In the book *Orthodoxy*, author G. K. Chesterton writes directly to the skeptic in this particular comment:

> It is we Christians who accept all actual evidence—it is you rationalists who refuse actual evidence being constrained to do so by your creed. But I am not constrained by any creed in the matter, and looking impartially into the miracles of medieval and modern times, I have come to the conclusion that they occurred.[17]

If Jesus is who He said He is, then it is not so incredible that He could heal a person. When a person cannot accept the miracles of Jesus, it is likely that the real problem is that they do not believe He was God in the flesh; they are "constrained by their creed" of atheism, agnosticism, scientific methodology, and so on to believe He was merely a man. The issue of Jesus' godhood will be addressed more in the next chapter. For now, suffice it to say, our belief in the miraculous is directly tied to our beliefs about God.

The issue of faith comes up during several of the healing miracles. Jesus often attributes the occurrence of the miracle to the person's faith. "Your faith has made you well" (Matt. 9:22); "Your faith has saved you" (Luke 7:50); "It shall be done for you as you have believed" (Matt. 8:13); "O woman, your faith is great; it shall be done for you as you wish" (Matt. 15:28). On the other hand, Mark 6:1–6 describes Jesus teaching in Nazareth. The people there are offended by Him, and verses 5–6 state, "He could do no miracle there except that He laid His hands on a few sick people and healed them. And He wondered at their unbelief." Quite a contrast to the other accounts in which it seems Jesus is impressed with the expressions of faith He encounters.

The question of belief is foundational to our relationship with God. God has made us to be free in the sense that He does not force us to believe in Him. He desires that we choose to put our faith and trust in Him. God remains partially hidden, leaving His fingerprints here and there. It requires faith and trust to relate to God, "...for who hopes for what he already sees?"(Rom. 8:24). Hebrews 11:6 speaks unflinchingly on this: "And *without faith it is impossible to please Him*, for who comes to God must believe that He is and that He is a rewarder of those who seek Him." So if you want to please God, you must believe that He exists and that He is a good God, even during those times when it doesn't *feel* like it's true. The difficulty is believing this truth in every situation, at all times, with no exceptions.

The two men in Matthew 9 did not waste time asking Jesus why they were blind or what they had done to deserve it. I appreciate the single-mindedness of the blind men. Even though it seemed that Jesus was ignoring them, they kept after Him. Does it ever seem to you that God is ignoring your request for a miracle? God does not ignore, but He does test. Do you believe that He is able to do what you are asking? Are you willing to keep believing despite all odds? Are you willing to wait for the answer? God tested Abraham by asking him to sacrifice his only son, and Abraham went ahead, assuming that God could raise Isaac from the dead. But God stopped Abraham from completing the sacrifice and said to him, "...now I know that you fear God" (Gen. 22:12).

Jesus asking the men the question was their test. They could have said, "We don't know for sure, but we're willing to give it a try. Nothing else has worked." This is how we approach the God of miracles many times—as a last resort. We often ask without really believing that God wants what is good for us, as though we must plead with God to give us good things. The problem is that our definition of "good things" usually needs some reworking to line up with God's definition. Jesus emphasizes the goodness of God and His desire to give good things to His children in Matthew 7:9–11: "Or what man is there among you who, when his son asks for a loaf, will give him a stone? Or if he asks for a fish, he will not give him a snake, will he? If you then, being evil, know how to give good gifts to your children, how much more will your Father who is in heaven give what is good to those who ask Him!"

Jesus wants to heal the people that come to Him, but He does not usually act against their own beliefs. Jesus does not perform the miracle so the person will begin to believe; rather, He acts in response to existing belief. The miracles strengthen the faith that is already in place, however weak or small it may have been. When Jesus asks the men if they believe, they answer a simple "yes." Jesus answers, "It shall be done to you according to your faith" (9:29), and they are healed immediately.

Sometimes our response is more like the father in Mark 9:24, who asks Jesus to heal his son. When Jesus tells him all things are possible to the one who believes, the father cries out, "I do believe; help my unbelief!" What a great prayer! "Lord, I do believe, but my faith is so small and my understanding of You is so limited; help me to rid myself of this unbelief and grab onto the truth that You are who You say You are." If you find that you cannot answer an enthusiastic "Yes!" when God asks if you believe, then offer Him the grain of faith you do have and ask Him to make it grow. If you find you have none at all, then offer that to Him. He will take that as your act of faith. It's not necessarily the "amount" of faith that is so important, but where you place it.

As Christians, we must believe in the God who does miracles. We have all thought or said at some point, "Oh, that won't change" or "He/she won't change" or "I can't change that." Since there are so many situations and people in our lives that make us feel powerless, we falsely assume that God is powerless as well. Most of the time we are powerless to heal our own bodies or to make someone see his or her own self-destructive behaviors. The two men knew they couldn't do anything about their eyes. Maybe they had been to every doctor and everyone had told them that it was hopeless and they should just let it go because nothing could be done.

But with God, all things are possible. Sarah laughed when the Lord told her she would have a son at the age of ninety, and God responded, "Is anything too hard for the Lord?" (Gen. 18:13–14). And, no, He is not a magic genie who answers our every wish. Sometimes the miracle is not what we expect. When we beg God to change our situation, often He changes us instead.

I have found this to be true in my own life. Every year there is at least one student whom I find difficult to love. This difficult student is usually lazy, fails to turn in any homework, lies, cheats, steals, or is disrespectful. I lose patience quickly and become frustrated. My first inclination is to pray and hope that the student changes…or moves away. However, I have noticed that this rarely happens. In fact, it is usually that student who has perfect attendance all year long. Most often it is my attitude towards the student that must change. Usually God gives me a glimpse into why this child is difficult to love, and I realize all over again that children are incredibly strong to survive the way they do. And of course I am confronted with the reality that quite often I am not that much easier to love than the student. It is miraculous to be able to see someone with new eyes, to have my heart and mind changed towards that person in such a way that I know it is not of myself. I am far from perfect at loving others, but I have learned to pray for this in my life.

We are quick to pray for physical healing or comforts, but slow to pray for our spiritual healing and renewal. Sometimes what God does on the inside is the greater and more difficult miracle than physical healing or comfort. It would not be surprising that a person would be able to praise God after miraculously recovering from an illness or receiving financial relief in an unexpected way. This is how God sometimes operates. Other times, the greater and more memorable miracles are when He gives peace and assurance in the midst of suffering and enables us to stand up under it. Perhaps it is easier to believe that God would raise the dead than give you strength, peace, and joy in the darkest times, yet God does both at the proper time.

Conclusion and Reflection

Believing is seeing. This means we don't see ourselves or our situations correctly until our beliefs are in order. "Seeing" cannot dictate belief, because we too easily forget what we have seen God accomplish. Remember the Israelites, who saw the hand of God deliver them from Egypt and then quickly turned to worship a golden calf? God shows Himself to those who believe that He is there and that He is good.

- What are you asking God to do in your life or the lives of the people around you?
- What do you do when you don't get your desired answer?
- How might God want to change you rather than change your circumstances?
- In what ways has God demonstrated His power and His presence in your life?
- How can praying the honest prayer, "Lord, I do believe; help my unbelief," change your approach to God?

QUESTION #6

MARK 8:29— "WHO DO YOU SAY THAT I AM?"

Who is Jesus? He lived two thousand years ago, in an obscure town, in an obscure country, during a relatively dark period in human history that was dominated by the Roman Empire. Yet He stands unequaled and unparalleled in the phenomenal greatness of His life as well as the stunning impact He has had on history.[18]

—from *Just Give Me Jesus*

THIS QUESTION SHOULD weigh on your heart every single day. After question 8, it is the most important one for you and me to answer well. Before you can answer or say anything of importance, you must decide your response to Jesus' question in Mark 8:29. Your response will ultimately lead to your salvation or your condemnation. This is the starting point (or ending point) of your Christian life: Who do you say Jesus is?

Context

Mark 8 begins with the account of Jesus feeding the 4,000, then tells of His healing of a blind man, and concludes with Jesus predicting His death and resurrection. It is not at all accidental that Jesus' question about who He is occurs in the midst of such events. Every word and action recorded by the gospel writers is meant to demonstrate that Jesus is the Messiah, the Son of the living God. Though the main point of Jesus' life on earth is to provide redemption, He is also demonstrating through His teaching and miracles what the kingdom of God is like. There will be no hunger (feeding the crowds), no disease (healing the sick), and no death (resurrection of the dead). This is the work and ministry of the Messiah.

Ultimately, the Messiah is a Savior and Redeemer. Consider Isaiah 53, a messianic prophecy delivered some 700 years before the birth of Christ. "He was despised and rejected by men…He took up our infirmities and carried our sorrows….He was pierced for our transgressions….After the suffering of His soul, He will see the light of life and be satisfied…For He bore the sin of many, and made intercession for the transgressors" (53:3–12). Jesus' miracles and teachings are not haphazard but intentional and direct in purpose—Jesus is the Messiah foretold by the prophets of God for hundreds of years.

The question of Jesus' identity takes on renewed depth within this context. It is not asked "out of the blue" or at the very beginning of Jesus' ministry. He waits a sufficient amount of time, giving the disciples the chance to observe and interact with Him personally. At the appropriate moment, Jesus asks, "Who do you say that I am?"

Digging Deeper

Peter answers this question by saying, "You are the Christ," but others had different opinions. The Pharisees are best known for their unfavorable view of Him. They said, "This man cast out demons only by Beelzebub the ruler of demons" (Matt. 12:24). They think of Jesus as a man possessed or empowered by Satan. Others believe He is Elijah, Jeremiah, John the Baptist, or some other prophet reincarnated (Matt. 16:14). Some, like the two blind men, refer to Him as the Son of David, Rabbi, or Lord. Then there is the criminal hanging on the cross next to Jesus. Luke records the man's words about Jesus in 23:41–42: "We indeed are suffering justly, for we are receiving what we deserve for our deeds; but this man has done nothing wrong.... Jesus, remember me when You come into your kingdom!" Though Jesus is badly beaten, bruised, bleeding, and near death, this man on the other cross recognizes that Jesus is the Savior of the whole world, including him. G. K. Chesterton describes Jesus and people's response to Him in this way:

> Suppose we hear an unknown man spoken of by many men. Suppose we were puzzled to hear that some men said he was too tall and some too short; some objected to his fatness, some lamented his leanness...some thought him too dark, and some too fair. One explanation...would be that he might be an odd shape. But there is another explanation. He might be the right shape.... Perhaps (in short) this extraordinary thing is really the ordinary thing; at least the normal thing, the centre.[19]

Before answering this question about who Jesus was and is for yourself, it might be helpful to see what Jesus said about Himself. John records several of Jesus' statements about Himself: "I am the Bread of Life" (6:48); "Before Abraham was born, I AM" (8:58); "I am the Light of the world" (9:5); "I am the Door" (10:9); "I am the good Shepherd" (10:14); "I and the Father are one" (10:30); "I am the Way, the Truth, and the Life; no one gets to the Father but through Me" (14:6); "I am the first and the last, and the living One; and I was dead, and behold, I am alive forevermore, and I have the keys of death and of Hades" (Rev. 1:17–18).

Jesus clearly views Himself as an equal with God the Father. The Gospels teach that He came to provide redemption, eternal life, protection, and guidance. There is an argument that states that Jesus must have been one of three things: a liar, a lunatic, or Lord (as He claimed to be). The argument makes the assertion that since Christ proved Himself to be truthful (not a liar) and rational (not crazy; just read the accounts of what He said and did), then the only option left is Lord. We can, therefore, draw the conclusion that Christ is indeed Lord. If He is truthful and rational in other areas, these characteristics should apply to His claims of Deity.[20]

However, these claims of Christ (especially John 14:6) are some of the most controversial aspects of Christianity today. For many people, truth is at best subjective to individual judgment or preference, and at worst, nonexistent. Most people believe in some form of moral relativism, which means you can't make your truth claims stick to other people. The general consensus is that you can believe anything you want—just keep it to yourself. In addition, there is the belief that all religions are basically the same and lead to the same place. This is the reasoning behind the tolerance mantra: as long as you aren't hurting anyone, do as you will, and do not insist that any person should think the same as you.

Jesus broke all of these rules, unapologetic when He stated that no one could be saved unless that person went through Him. There are not many truths; there are not many ways to the truth. There is only One, and that is Jesus. Making this claim today is begging for a fight, yet it is as true now as it was when Jesus said it, even in the midst of pluralism. Jesus warned that we would be hated, just as He was. We will be hated because people want to attain salvation on their own terms. We often want to deny who Jesus is so we don't have to change our lives.

An eight-year-old student once asked me, "Why did they kill Jesus?" It was a worthy question, which I had to think about. The answer is found in Matthew 13:57a: "And they took offense at Him." The people were offended by Jesus then just as much as they are now. He is the stumbling block, full of irony and contradiction. His is the vagrant carpenter, claiming to be the Son of God. He is the uneducated preacher who socialized with the outcasts, tax collectors, and Gentiles. He performs miraculous signs, yet disregards the rigid Sabbath rules. But worst of all, He takes away every reason people have for thinking of themselves as worthy of salvation. Anne Graham Lotz describes Jesus in this way in her book *Just Give Me Jesus*:

> Who is Jesus? He lived two thousand years ago, in an obscure town, in an obscure country, during a relatively dark period in human history that was dominated by the Roman Empire. Yet He stands unequaled and unparalleled in the phenomenal greatness of His life as well as the stunning impact He has had on history.[21]

Christian author and church leader Watchman Nee was falsely accused and imprisoned during the rise of communism in China. After Nee's death in prison, a note was found under his pillow, which said: "Christ is the Son of God who died for the redemption of sinners and resurrected after three days. This is the greatest truth in the universe. I die because of my belief in Christ."[22] The issue of Christ's identity is literally a matter of life and death, not just for Christ, but for anyone who follows Him.

Today He still abolishes ideologies that attempt to replace God rather than honor Him. He is offensive to us because He insists we look away from ourselves, even to the point of death, in order to embrace the life that is found only in Him. He demands we give up ourselves, when we would rather protect ourselves. He calls us to repent, when we would rather justify our actions. He says that redemption is our most urgent need, when we would rather be comfortable. He steps on our toes without apology. Yet Jesus said, "Blessed is he who does not take offense at Me" (Luke 7:23).

If you have never been offended by Jesus, then you haven't listened closely and taken His teachings to heart. If you have been offended but never moved from your offense, then you must go deeper still. This narrow path will eventually lead you to the realization that it is not God who is offensive or contradictory; it is you, it is me, it is all of humanity.

Jesus called Himself the door through which we must pass to be saved. That doorway is so narrow that few will humble themselves enough to pass through it. People are put off by the fact that they don't seem to fit. They think the doorway should expand to accommodate them. Others decide to squeeze through and discover much of themselves getting scraped off in the process. We stumble over Jesus because of who we are in contrast to Him. When we are offended and stumble often, we look for other ways and methods to attain our salvation.

Non-Christians are certainly not the only ones looking for alternative routes. Each of us in our own way seeks circuitous paths to avoid our Maker. Religion is plagued with these attempts. We look to our good works, our intentions, our church attendance, our Bible studies, and countless other religious activities we are called upon to do. Yet these acts are not our salvation or righteousness, nor are they even truth in and of themselves. We grab hold of these things we do and point to them as evidence of our righteousness, because if we can be righteous by our deeds, then there is no need for a Savior. This is our human-centered default religion. Christ becomes obsolete and we are free, at least by our own perception. Strangely, we often perceive Christ as our captor, the One holding the scourge and keeping us from being truly free. This is the lie from the world that freedom only comes when there is no accountability and no power or authority greater than yourself.

Jesus' statement in John 14:6 is not meant to be a stranglehold, but rather a calling for those with ears to listen. It is a difficult teaching for our stubborn and rebellious hearts. In order to take hold of Jesus' words, there must be humility and relinquishing of self-righteousness. Surprisingly, we are promised that we will find freedom, and even greatness, in humility. Do not make apologies to the world for Jesus' bold words, for His are the only words of truth and life in a world that is covered in darkness and starving for hope.

I appreciate Peter's boldness in answering Jesus' question: "You are the Christ." Yet these are only words. I don't believe that when Jesus asks us this important question that He is only listening for the right words; He is looking for the right actions. When you give your true answer to whom Jesus is, it will be with your actions. Your actions will give away what you really believe about the identity of Christ and what it means to you. You will answer with the way in which you live your life, not just in one day but in the summation of your days. What does your life say about who Jesus was and is? Does it say He is irrelevant? Does it say He is Lord? Does it say He is in every part or just there on Sundays? Or maybe just at the most difficult times?

As I stated above, Peter has the right words. However, later on in the passage it is clear that Peter doesn't have the right understanding of who the Christ is and what He is supposed to do. Peter calls Jesus "the Christ," but he doesn't know what it really means because he has false knowledge. It was the common belief of the Jews at that time that the Messiah would be a political hero who would overthrow the Romans and reestablish the kingdom of Israel to its former glory, as it was under King David. Therefore, in the gospel accounts, when Jesus talks about suffering and dying, Peter is horrified. Many times Jesus tries to correct the disciples' misunderstanding, but it does not make sense to them. It isn't until after Jesus rises from the dead, speaks to them, and sends the Holy Spirit to indwell them that they finally understand Jesus' purpose.

It is much the same for us. Understanding who Jesus was and is will be a lifelong pursuit. Our beliefs about Him must be continuously refined and deepened. It's like Job's experience of first hearing about God, then seeing Him personally. As beliefs are deepened, lives will become transformed. Romans 12:1 says that we are transformed by the renewing of our minds, which will in turn transform our beliefs so that they conform to the Truth. Philip Yancey wrote a book titled *The Jesus I Never Knew*, in which he chronicles his ongoing journey in learning the truth about who Jesus was and is. He writes, "According to Jesus, what I think about Him and how I respond will determine my destiny for all eternity."[23] In other words, truth matters.

Genuine truth will define and describe reality in an objective manner. Many Christians unintentionally separate the truth from their reality, thinking that the Bible (Truth) has no place in reality. When it comes down to the wire, who wants to be in possession of beliefs you knew were worthless? Strangely, people are willing to risk this.

The bottom line is that truth is real and available to us, and it demands to be reckoned with. Matthew notes several of Jesus' run-ins with the religious leaders. During an episode referred to earlier, in Matthew 12, the leaders accused Jesus of casting out demons by the power of Satan. In the heat of the moment, maybe this sounded rational and even probable, just as many ridiculous and self-contradictory things can sound at first. But Jesus holds up a mirror for them, and He asks, "How can Satan cast out Satan?" In other words, why would Satan cast himself out and thereby be counterproductive? What the Pharisees try to use as evidence against Jesus' miracles is illogical. He reveals that they are not really after truth or justice in this matter, but rather that they are attempting to explain an event without acknowledging the power of God. In their attempt to explain what happened without accepting Christ, they sound foolish and ignorant.

Then there is Matthew 12:28, which comes across as a verbal punch in the stomach. After Jesus has just discredited the Pharisees' only explanation for the miraculous events, He says, "But if I cast out demons by the Spirit of God, then the kingdom of God has come upon you." Jesus is saying to the world then and now, "You had better pay attention to what you believe about Me." The path of truth is found only in Christ, and we must reconcile ourselves to this or face a world of incongruity. My worldview must be wrapped around the truth of Christ, because having it any other way will lead to a cave-in.

So it comes to the driving question behind the Gospels, or perhaps the entire Bible. What are you going to do with Jesus? Ephesians 1:9–10 reads, "He made known to us the mystery of His will, according to His kind intention which He purposed in Him with a view to an administration suitable to the fullness of the times, that is, *the summing up of all things in Christ*, things in the heavens and on the earth." That phrase, "…the summing up of all things in Christ," is as powerful as it is revealing. Paul is saying that all things have built up to the moment of His appearance on earth. *"All things"* includes the act of creation, the fall, separation, suffering, blood sacrifices, war, the tabernacle, the temple, exile, the destruction of Israel, the rebuilding of Israel, and every person along the way who knowingly or unknowingly became a part of the great narrative leading up to Christ. He is the summing up of all these things, from the past up to what is yet to come. There is nothing in heaven or on earth that Jesus does not touch or answer.

One of my favorite verses is John 1:14: "And the Word [Jesus] became flesh and dwelt [literally translated, 'tabernacled'] among us, and we saw His glory, glory as of the only begotten from the Father, full of grace and truth." God became man so that He might come nearer to us and we to Him. He walked, talked, ate, slept, laughed, cried, suffered, bled, and died; He lived among us as one of us. He became the face and voice of God that we could see and hear without perishing. Hebrews 4:14–16 explains why He did this:

> Therefore, since we have a great high priest who has passed through the heavens, Jesus the Son of God, let us hold fast our confession. For we do not have a high priest who cannot sympathize with our weaknesses, but One who has been tempted in all things as we are, yet without sin. Therefore, let us draw near with confidence to the throne of grace, so that we may receive mercy and find grace to help in time of need.

In summary, then, who is this Christ that is in us? He is the Son of God, the Messiah, as foretold in the Old Testament (Gen. 3:15; Matt. 3:17). He is the One who created the universe and all things in it (John 1:3), including mankind, knowing even then that we would not choose Him first. He humiliated Himself before His own rebellious creation, being subjected to what we do to our worst of criminals (Phil. 2:8; Mark 15; and Matt. 27). He willingly made Himself small and tangible and suffered the ailments of human existence so we would know God and relate to Him and He to us (John 1:14; Matt. 4). He got down on His knees and lived among us in the dirt, allowing us to look on Him and hear Him and touch Him (Luke 24:39; Mark 9:7).

He did not chastise us for making Him come down, but rather He loved us in such a way that we might be raised up (Matt. 11:28–30). He loved us with such ferociousness that death itself was reversed (1 Cor. 15:55–57), the curtain was torn (Matt. 27:51), and the gap was bridged (Ezek. 22:30–31). He loved us that we might love Him in return, because He knew this was the only way we could be fulfilled (Rom. 5:5–6). He knew this and acted on our behalf, though we did not ask or invite Him to do so (Eph. 2:4–5). He has loved us because of who He is, not who we are (Deut. 7:7–9).

He is the Bread of Life, the Light of the World, and the sacrificial Lamb who came to take away the sins of the world. He is the fulfillment of ancient prophecy (Matt. 1:22–23, 2:6, 17–18; Is. 9:6–7) and the summing up of all things, past, present, and future (Eph. 1:10). He is our hope of salvation, our hope of glory, our hope that the best is yet to come. We need not fear that He will change or depart from us, for He has promised to be with us to the very end of the age (Matt. 28:20b). This is the Christ who indwells us and who loves us with unspeakable love.

Conclusion and Reflection

If you have done a cursory reading of His teachings, then you have perhaps learned enough to be dangerous to yourself and those around you. If you apply His teaching here and there, then you have done better than many. If you believe He is who He said He is, then you have received a revelation that will impact every aspect of your life. Should you choose to ignore the truth of Christ, I challenge you to try to live consistently with this belief. The same challenge stands even more so for those who embrace Him.

- Who is Jesus in your daily life?
- Who is Jesus as revealed in the Bible?
- How do your beliefs about Jesus impact your actions and thoughts each day?
- What beliefs need to be transformed?
- Are you hesitant or ashamed to claim that Jesus is the *only* way to salvation and the *only* truth?

QUESTION #7

LUKE 24:17— "WHAT ARE YOU DISCUSSING TOGETHER AS YOU WALK ALONG?"

> And no man can be a rhapsode who does not understand the meaning of the poet. For the rhapsode ought to interpret the mind of the poet to his hearers, but how can he interpret him well unless he knows what he means?[24]
> —from *The Dialogues of Plato*

THE CONTEXT OF this question (Luke 24:13–35) demonstrates one key aspect of Jesus' ministry. Christ came to bring salvation, truth, and life, but He did it by *intervention*. It would have been logically possible for God to have devised a plan in which we were not informed or involved in what happened. God could have waived His mercy and consigned everyone to hell or waived His judgment and allowed everyone into heaven. However, God does not compromise His character. Instead, He sent Jesus. Jesus, in the very act of taking on the human form, intervened in human history. He lived, moved, spoke, and acted among us in such a way that it interrupted the flow of our lives. Some stumbled over Him, some cursed Him, and some were confused or enraged. Others were saved.

If we are to be saved, God must be the one to do something because we are powerless to attain salvation on our own. It is God's nature to intervene in our lives, even in our thoughts and conversations.

Context

In Luke 24 the resurrected Jesus does not deviate from this plan of intervention. His mission is to bring truth, understanding, and salvation. Luke tells us that two men were walking on the road to Emmaus (about seven miles west of Jerusalem) and talking about all the things that had happened concerning Jesus the past few days. Then Jesus was there, walking with them, but they didn't recognize Him. He asked, "What are you discussing together as you walk along?" (24:17). The men are obviously shocked that this man hadn't heard all of what happened. Imagine if someone had asked you about the O. J. Simpson trial or the 9/11 terrorist attacks while they were happening. How can you not know what happened? Out of what hole did you just crawl?

They proceeded to tell the man about Jesus the prophet and how He was sentenced to death by the chief priests and rulers (24:19–20). The men revealed their expectations in verse 21, stating one of the greatest ironies recorded in Scripture: "But we were hoping that it was He who was going to redeem Israel." They also reported that some women had been to Jesus' tomb earlier that morning and found that it was empty. The women claimed that He is alive, which is understandably troubling for the others to believe. Jesus then called the two men foolish and slow to believe in the things the prophets said: "Was it not necessary for the Christ to suffer these things and to enter into His glory?" (24:26). Yet another key question.

Digging Deeper

Jesus' point in interrupting the men's conversation was ultimately to correct their thinking and lead them to salvation.

They, like most of the Jews, had a false understanding of the Messiah. They would never have conceived of a Messiah who would suffer and die for the sins of the whole world. Their plan was for the Messiah to overthrow Rome and establish Israel as the prominent nation it once was under King David, but they had misread and misunderstood the promises and revelations of God. It was not until Jesus rose from the dead and visited His followers that a few people began to understand the Scriptures. Even then, many did not believe, and today most Jews still await the coming of the Messiah.

Some might feel that having correct beliefs about spiritual or religious matters is not important. However, correct thinking is not just preferable; it is necessary. It is your thoughts and beliefs that guide your actions. Therefore, believing a lie is equivalent to living a lie. We believe a lie and then build our lives around it. We believe we are righteous on our own, that there is no God, that our sins are not that bad, that God is not that good, that God cannot be trusted, and that people cannot be trusted. One or more of these beliefs might lie at the core of your mind and soul. If that is so, then the rest of your beliefs, and ultimately your actions, will be motivated by that core belief or beliefs.

Much of Jesus' teaching ministry focused not on outward behaviors but on intrinsic motivations, beliefs, thoughts, and so on. Look at the Sermon on the Mount. In Matthew 5:21–48 Jesus gave a series of commands, following a certain pattern. He said something like, "You have heard it said to you…." and then added, "But now I say to you…." Where the Old Testament law focused on the outward behaviors, Jesus shined the light on the inner self. Consider these teachings of Jesus from Matthew 5:

> You have heard that the ancients were told, "You shall not commit murder," …but I say to you that everyone who is angry with his brother shall be guilty before the court. (5:21–22)

> You have heard that is was said, "You shall not commit adultery," but I say to you that everyone who looks at a women with lust for her has already committed adultery with her in his heart. (5:27–28)
>
> You have heard that it was said, "An eye for an eye, and tooth for a tooth." But I say to you, do not resist and evil person; but whoever slaps you on your right cheek, turn the other to him also. (5:38–39)

The men walking on the road to Emmaus thought the redemption of Israel meant political freedom, but Jesus was really there to redeem them from their own sin. This kind of misunderstanding of Jesus' mission and ministry is not exclusive to the first-century Jews. It can wind up being the same for you and me. God will call attention to our false beliefs and the conversations we have based on them.

In my junior year of college there was a job I wanted very much. It fit me perfectly as far as my abilities and previous job experience, plus the pay was more than I had been getting. However, this position was normally reserved for graduate students, and I would only be a senior. One day in the library I was praying about it again, begging God to allow me to have this job. I was convinced that it was the best thing for me and equally worried that God would deny me something good. I prayed almost out loud, "Lord, if you would allow me to have this job, I would praise you so much." Just as the words entered my mind, the Lord answered back, "Would you praise me just as much if you did not get the job?"

The question hit me like a load of wet towels. God was calling my attention to the conversation. His question forced me to think about my words and to see my incongruity. I had to go back over what I had said to Him and reorder my beliefs. I believed that I knew what was best for me and that if I wanted it badly enough I might get it. I also believed that it would make me happy and that if I were happy I would be more inclined to give praise to God.

The truth that is you and I don't know what is best, even for ourselves. In addition, it is not always true that we praise God most during the good times. Even so, true worship and devotion are not contingent on outward circumstances but are based on continuous trust. I didn't get the job for that following year, and I wound up staying in my position as a resident assistant.

At the halfway point through my third year of being a resident assistant in the dormitory, I had a quasi-meltdown. I was so burned out that I couldn't see straight anymore. I felt like I was unraveling mentally, emotionally, and spiritually. Many of the things that used to come so easily for me—like Bible reading, prayer, church, friendships, and school work—now seemed impossible. This went on until December, when I thought I couldn't continue this way any longer.

One night in my room I just started venting to God about everything I felt: all my frustrations, how I hated being a resident assistant, and on and on. I kept talking and carrying on because I didn't want to stop and listen, but it finally got to a point when I didn't have anything more to say, and I decided to try listening. It was as though I had emptied myself of everything I had been carrying and now I was ready to be filled. When I calmed down, I asked God, "Why did you take those things away from me?" I was referring to all those things I used to do so well, or so I thought. He said to me, "Because those things are not your righteousness."

I remember sitting there stunned. I had honestly thought there was nothing He could say to me that would shed light on the situation or change my feelings. Not only is this a false belief, but also it revealed one of my core beliefs—that my righteousness was defined mostly by my actions.

God is deeply concerned and invested in our beliefs. He wants us to believe and think according to truth, because He knows it is in our best interest. Jesus taught that it is not what goes into a person that defiles, but what comes out (Matt. 15:11). The things we say and do reflect what is in our hearts and minds. God asks us, "What are you thinking about? What are you talking about to yourself and to others? What do you believe about Me?" He does this to get us to reflect and to respond.

Often when you say it out loud or see it in writing, the false belief becomes more obvious, and therefore more difficult to believe. This is one of the many reasons we are told to remain in fellowship with other Christians. We can sharpen and correct each other in regard to the truth. "Iron sharpens iron, so one man sharpens another" (Prov. 27:17). Also, many people find it helpful to journal their thoughts and experiences. Somehow it's more difficult to lie to yourself in writing. For years I have kept a journal or expressed myself in writing, some of it on these very pages. So many times I was sure that I could easily articulate a particular thought or belief, only to find out that it was not the case. It has taken me much time and energy to think through and express my faith, and I am far from finished. Whether through fellowship or writing or prayer, the objective is to eradicate the lies and buttress the truth in our thoughts and actions.

After God confronted me, I realized I had thought all along that I was above that kind of false thinking. I knew what the Bible taught and that salvation was by grace through faith. Precisely when I think I am exempt is when I fall into the trap. It was a humbling experience to realize that I had stepped into such an obvious quagmire, yet I was grateful it was brought to my attention.

At times, God can work in that quiet and subtle way. It's almost humorous the way Jesus played the part of the naive stranger in Luke 24. He insisted that the men explain everything from their perspective, although He already knew what they would say. Why would He do this? Why not just come right out and say that they had been wrong from the beginning? There is no way to know for certain because Luke does not say why.

However, reading the context of the narrative and having an understanding of human nature may bring some insight. Jesus wanted them to explain it, not so He could hear it, but so *they* could hear it. We have all had the experience of being deeply involved in some conversation about something that has been going on for a while. Suddenly, someone new comes along and you have to explain everything from the beginning. This makes you put all the pieces that you have together so that it can be told in a coherent way. Through that process, you might even think of things that you had not considered before. It causes you to step back and see a larger picture.

Jesus was that new person who came along asking, "What are you talking about?" So they told Him everything they knew up to that point, and in the process, they relived their heartache, disappointment, and confusion. I can just imagine that they felt so empty after retelling the events. They were probably begging God in their hearts to make sense of all this mess, just as I remember doing in my dorm room that December night. It's frightening coming to the end of your narrative; it's like standing at the edge of a precipice. Only after telling your side of it do you realize how empty it is without God.

Isn't this how we vent? When we vent to God—our frustration, anger, hurt, pain—we tell the story from our end, as though God were not in it, and it is a bitter story to tell. Just go back and read the Psalms. But I have seen that often I am not willing to hear God's version until I have told mine. God understands this about me. And when I tell my story He takes it, nods His head, and then offers His side. C. S. Lewis captures this in his masterpiece *Til We Have Faces*:

> When the time comes to you at which you will be forced at last to utter the speech which has lain at the center of your soul for years, which you have, all that time, idiot-like, been saying over and over, you'll not talk about joy of words. I saw well why the gods do not speak to us openly, nor let us answer. Till that word can be dug out of us, why should they hear the babble that we think we mean? How can they meet us face to face till we have faces? [25]

This is exactly what happened with the two men on the road to Emmaus. They finished telling what they knew, and Jesus told them they had failed to understand what the prophets said about the Messiah. He proceeded to retell the great Narrative, pointing out to them how the Scriptures foretold who and what the Messiah would be. It would be fascinating to know what exactly Jesus said to those men, to know what Scriptures He referenced and how He tied it all together. One thing is certain—He made it clear that the Messiah came to pay the penalty for sin in a way no animal sacrifice or human action ever could. It is also certain that those men never had heard that kind of teaching before, yet they didn't pick up stones to kill Him. In fact, they invited Jesus to stay longer with them.

It was no accident that Jesus revealed Himself to these men at that time. They were at the height of their disappointment. Before His crucifixion, whenever Jesus would tell His followers about His suffering and death, they either refused to hear it or were simply confused. As I said before, there was no room for a suffering or dead Messiah in their worldview, but now that they thought Jesus was dead, room was being made. They were able to finally hear Jesus tell about Himself because their prior beliefs were in shambles. They handed Jesus these broken pieces of their story, and He wove them together in such a way that it formed an intricate mosaic, every piece held in place by the pieces around it. No one had foreseen how the story would unfold, and only Jesus could tell it.

The problem is that we often see God's story as foolish. We may not use those words, but we reveal these thoughts in our actions. We become so tangled in our own interpretation of reality that anything else seems less real. Saint Augustine once stated, "We are ensnared by the wisdom of the serpent; we are set free by the foolishness of God." Obviously Satan is not "wise" and God is not "foolish," but Augustine's quote is meant to point out the way we often see things in our arrogance and ignorance. Paul writes in 1 Corinthians 1:18–25:

> I know very well how foolish the message of the cross sounds to those who are on the road to destruction. But we who are being saved recognize this message as the very power of God.... Since God in his wisdom saw to it that the world would never find him through human wisdom, he has used our foolish preaching to save all who believe.... So when we preach that Christ was crucified, the Jews are offended, and the Gentiles say it is all nonsense. But to those called by God to salvation, both Jews and Gentiles, Christ is the mighty power of God and wonderful wisdom of God. This "foolish" plan of God is far wiser than the wisest of human plans, and God's weakness is far stronger than the greatest of human strength. (NLT)

Paul talked about the Jews and Gentiles, but we deal with a different crowd. In our culture, the two extremes are represented by those who believe all religions are true and lead to God (called the religious pluralists) and those who believe there is no God or gods at all (atheist or agnostic). I put 1 Corinthians 1:23–24 into our modern setting:

> God's way of offering salvation by grace through Christ is offensive to those of other religions or those who claim all religions are ways to truth. On the other hand, Christ's offer of salvation appears to be complete nonsense to the atheist. So while it is offensive to the religious pluralist and ridiculous to the atheist, for those who are being saved, Christ is the power and the wisdom of God.

The truth of God is interpreted by people in different ways, yet it is God's desire that we accept it as it is. The men Jesus questioned thought they had all the pieces to understand God's truth until Jesus engaged them in a dialogue. The wisdom to understand God and His truth will only come once we are willing to listen and become participants on God's terms.

In one Socratic dialogue, Socrates is conversing with a man named Ion, who is a rhapsode (one who recited or performed poetry). Socrates is concerned about the art of interpretation and poses this statement to Ion:

> And no man can be a rhapsode who does not understand the meaning of the poet. For the rhapsode ought to interpret the mind of the poet to his hearers, but how can he interpret him well unless he knows what he means?[26]

This quote struck me because the word "rhapsode" can be substituted with "Christian" and "poet" with "God." Then the quote would read this way:

> And no man can be a Christian who does not understand the meaning of God. For the Christian ought to interpret the mind of God to his hearers, but how can the Christian interpret God well unless he knows what God means?

God is the great Poet, and we are the mere interpreters and partakers in His poetry. It is our joy and our purpose to seek out the Poet and to be a witness for Him to others. This was Jesus' purpose for sharing what He did with those men. He interpreted for them what God meant by sending the Messiah, thereby giving them a new and better story to tell.

When God asks you what you are talking about, go back and tell Him your story. Do not hold back, thinking He already knows, for the telling is not for His sake. Do not hold back, thinking there is nothing new to add, for only God sees the whole story. Do not hold back out of spite and anger toward God, for those emotions are also just a part of the story. When you finish telling your side, though, be ready to listen. He may tell you to wait; He may tell you only a little. He reveals to us what we can handle and understand at the time. Just like the disciples, you and I are merely a part of a great mosaic, a meta-narrative, being woven and fitted together by the master storyteller. Be ready to learn your part and live it well, no matter how small it may seem to you.

In the third book of the Narnia series, *The Horse and His Boy*, a young horse named Bree is worried about returning to Narnia after so long an absence. He fears he won't be as special anymore because he will no longer be the only talking horse. An old hermit says to Bree:

> You're not quite the great Horse you had come to think, from living among poor dumb horses. Of course you were braver and cleverer than them. You could hardly help being that. It doesn't follow that you'll be anyone very special in Narnia. But as long as you know you're nobody very special, you'll be a very decent sort of Horse.[27]

This is how it can be for us. You may not be as special as you once thought, or significant in the way you would like to think, but that is only because it is not your story to tell as you please.

Conclusion and Reflection

When God asks, "What are you talking about as you walk along?" stop and examine the story you are telling. Each of us has a running narrative in our minds, a framework from which we view ourselves, others, and God. When this framework gets distorted by self-centeredness, it becomes impossible to see or understand anything properly. As C. S. Lewis pointed out, Christianity is the meta-narrative by which all other things are understood.

- Who is at the center of your life-narrative?
- What tasks has God called you to do in this life?
- Do you listen when God is telling His side, or do you find yourself doing all the talking?
- What kinds of things do you tell yourself, others, and God?
- Do you see or hear the story that God tells as a whole or in fractured pieces?
- How does God see you and the part you play in His script?
- How do you see yourself?

QUESTION #8

JOHN 1:38— "WHAT DO YOU SEEK?"

"You have knocked at every door?" she asked.
"Yes."
"Have you knocked at that one there?"
"No."
"Knock there."[28]

—from *Les Miserables*

IF I HAD to choose which question was the most important, this would be the one. I would even go so far as to say that all other questions are subject to this question. I imagine this question going hand in hand with question 6. A conversation between Jesus and me might go like this: Jesus asks, "What do you seek?" I respond, "You, Lord." He asks, "And who do you say that I am?" I respond again, "You are the Christ, the Son of God." The answer to the first question determines whether the second question gets asked. The first question is more general, while the second question is more specific. Your answer to the first question will determine how you spend your life, for our lives are shaped by what we seek.

Context

The first chapter of John begins with a familiar phrase: "In the beginning..." (see Genesis 1:1). John takes the reader all the way back to the beginning to establish the important fact of Jesus' preexistence and equality with God. Jesus is identified as the fulfillment of the Old Testament law (1:17) and God in the flesh (1:14). In 1:19 the text turns to John the Baptist, who was baptizing and preaching about the coming of the One who would baptize in the Holy Spirit.

One day Jesus walked by John, and John said, "Behold, the Lamb of God who takes away the sin of the world!" This title, "Lamb of God," is another messianic term reflecting back to the Passover. The book of Exodus records the events surrounding the Passover and its significance. In Exodus 12 the Israelites are told to prepare a Passover supper in which the blood of a lamb is to be placed over the doorposts of every household. The blood will ensure that the plague on the firstborn will pass over that house. Jesus, the Lamb of God, has come to spill His blood to ensure that the wrath of God will pass over us at the time of judgment. John the Baptist's proclamation in 1:29 is entrenched with meaning, and he goes even further to say, "I have seen and I testify that this is the Son of God" (1:34).

The next day John is with two of his disciples, and when Jesus passes by, John calls out again, "Behold the Lamb of God!" The two disciples hear this and follow after Jesus. "And Jesus turned and saw them following and said to them, 'What do you seek?'" (1:38). The men ask where Jesus is staying, so Jesus invites them over, and they stay with Jesus for the day. Later, one of the men, Andrew, finds his brother, Peter, and tells him, "We have found the Messiah." Those men and others follow Jesus to the end of their lives.

Digging Deeper

[handwritten note: See Acts 17:22-31 / Mt. 28:20]

The concept of seeking, even the specific word, is found throughout Scripture. God is extremely concerned with what we seek. He designed us to be in fellowship with Him; therefore, we are hardwired to desire that fellowship and to seek after Him. Paul said in Athens to the pagan philosophers, "He himself gives life and breath to everything, and he satisfies every need there is.... His purpose in all of this was that the nations should *seek after God* and perhaps feel their way toward him and find him—though he is not far from any one of us" (see Acts 17:22–31).

Ecclesiastes 3:11 states, "God has made everything beautiful for its own time. He has planted eternity in the human heart...." God made us to live eternally with Him. However, due to sin and free will we fill that desire with other things. Everyone seeks to fill the void in some way or another. We often seek the quickest and easiest way, thus becoming a slave to our desires.

In Jeremiah 2, God reprimands Israel for leaving Him to chase after false gods. He is grieved by their unfaithfulness. "Yet My people have exchanged their glorious God for worthless idols! The heavens are shocked at such a thing and shrink back in horror and dismay.... My people have done two evil things: They have forsaken Me—the fountain of living water. And they have dug for themselves cracked cisterns that can hold no water at all!" (2:11b–13). They seek God, but they quickly leave Him to seek something else. Second Kings 17 describes the tragic exile of Israel due to their sins. Second Kings 17:15 explains what led to their defeat: "And they followed vanity and became vain." The people chase after that which is empty and become empty themselves. They seek to be free from Yahweh, but they find that this only leads to slavery.

Whatever you desire will rule over you, along with whatever you fear. Fear pushes you from behind, while desire hangs in front. I find that I can desire and fear the same thing. I desire to be close to people and develop friendships, but I am compelled by fear to pull away at times. It's a constant battle that must be kept in check. The only way to live a coherent and full life is to desire and fear God alone. For more about fear, see chapter 1. The remainder of this chapter will focus on desire, or what we seek.

The book of Ecclesiastes is a thoughtful and honest approach to the question of the meaning of life and of what we seek. The writer, commonly believed to be King Solomon, chips away all the candy coating and forces the reader to consider life as it would be without God. In trying to find meaning in life, Solomon begs the question, does what you seek justify the space you take and the air you breathe for however many years you might live? Solomon begins with a less than optimistic answer, stating, "Everything is meaningless" (1:2). However, being the good philosopher and social scientist, Solomon tries to find meaning in several aspects of life rather than just making casual observations. He conducts his own philosophical investigations and social experiments.

First, he seeks after wisdom and understanding and tries to distinguish wisdom from foolishness. God even makes him wiser than any other king before him; yet, this is ultimately unsatisfying. He observes, "Now I realize that even this was like chasing the wind. For the greater my wisdom, the greater my grief. To increase knowledge only increases sorrow" (1:17b–18).

Next he goes after pleasure. "I said to myself, 'Come now, let's give pleasure a try. Let's look for the good things in life.' But I found that this too was meaningless" (2:1). He drinks wine and laughs but finds it to be silly. He builds huge homes, gardens, parks, and acquires many slaves, singers, and concubines. He owns large herds and flocks of animals and collects piles of gold, silver, and other treasures. Solomon has everything that anyone could ever want—wealth, possessions, companions, greatness, wisdom. "But as I looked at everything I had worked so hard to accomplish, it was all so meaningless" (2:11a).

Solomon determines that everything is ultimately futile. The fruits of one's hard work will eventually be left to someone else to enjoy. The evil and the righteous, even the animals, share the same fate of death. He struggles with the suffering, evil, and injustice that he sees and thinks, "The dead are better off than the living. And most fortunate of all are those who were never born. For they have never seen all the evil that is done in our world" (4:2–3). In a world without God, there can be no justice, for everything would be left to random chance. In a world without God, you would be most wise to spend your days for yourself, to seek after your own happiness and pleasure while you can because your time is so short. But you will find, as Solomon did, that living for yourself is empty and inhumane. We cannot truly live as if there is no God because there is a God and He must come first.

When I was in high school, I remember my mom having a talk with me about the music I listened to and the people whose pictures hung on my wall. I asked her how I would know what was OK and what wasn't. I will never forget what she said to me: "Love God first, then do whatever you want." I was floored initially, because all I really heard was, "Do whatever you want." But when I actually stopped to consider these words, I understood their gravity. If I truly love God first, then what I want will come under submission to that love. It's not, "Do whatever you want, then love God." This is disastrous, yet it's what many of us do in our walks with God.

As an adult, this has meant more than examining my music. What career should I pursue? Love God first, and then do what you want. Should I pursue marriage or remain single? Love God first, and then do what you want. I have lost many hours of sleep and filled many journal pages trying to seek answers to those big decisions in life. Some decisions have been agonizing as I've examine the long-term ramifications. I don't find that God is always quick to send an answer. He longs for me to seek Him and desire Him even more than the answer to my question.

The desires we have in this life must come under submission to the highest desire—God Himself. Jesus says in Matthew 6:32–33, "…for your heavenly Father knows that you need all these things [food, clothing, and so on]. *But seek first His kingdom* and His righteousness and all these things will be added to you."

"Seek first His kingdom" means that the things of God should take preeminence among the things we seek. Notice that it is not the only thing we are to seek. However, when we are seeking God first, everything else will be put into proper perspective. In the context, Jesus is talking about anxiety and reassuring the listeners that the Father will take care of them and their needs. Worry comes when we begin to believe our needs will not be met and we must do something about it ourselves. Jesus says that we should not be preoccupied with seeking our own needs but instead seek the One who is greater than we are.

So what is the kingdom of God, and why must we seek it first, above all else? Jesus spends much of His time talking about the kingdom of God; a careful reading of the Gospels may even lead you to conclude that it is the dominant theme and topic of Jesus' teaching. There are two characteristics of the kingdom of God in Jesus' teachings that go hand in hand. The first is that the kingdom is hidden, and second, that it is of great value. Several of the parables, especially in Matthew 13, liken the kingdom to something valuable (treasures, a pearl) or influential (yeast), and yet in the analogy these things are not entirely apparent at first.

The theme of "hiddenness" is evident in the parable of the weeds and the wheat (Matt. 13:24–30). The two remain together in the field until the harvest, just as the good and evil coexist until the end of the age. During the time of cohabitation (which we are in now), we live in a shadow of what is to come. Just as gold must be heated to remove the impurities (yet the substance of the gold is always present), so must the kingdom be purged of evil. And just as impure gold might be overlooked or only have a faint resemblance to pure gold, the same is true for the kingdom of God right now.

The parables of the mustard seed and the yeast liken the kingdom to something that seems small and insignificant, yet it grows and shows itself to be influential. Jesus compares the kingdom to a small seed, which then grows into a large tree. His main point seems to be that looks can be deceiving. For a time it may appear small and hidden, but it is becoming, and will soon be, the largest of kingdoms.

The parables of the hidden treasure and the costly pearl continue the theme of hiddenness, but also they add the implication of the costliness and value of the kingdom. Why is the kingdom of God not like a castle on a hill? Or a vast gold mine? Instead, in both stories the kingdom seems to be of small size and something that is not immediately obvious but that must be sought out. Yet it is worth selling everything you or I have to gain this treasure.

Seeking His kingdom first demands that we live in obscurity, dead to ourselves, yielded, humbled, and hidden in Him. We must be in the world, mixed in with the weeds, yet remain as wheat (Matt. 13:24–30). But the weight of the treasure we will gain far outweighs everything else. This is Paul's message in 2 Corinthians 4:17: the suffering we experience now is light and fleeting compared to the surpassing weight of glory.

This speaks against our natural tendencies to demand recognition, attention, and glory now and for ourselves. Colossians 3:3–4 reads: "For you have died and *your life is hidden* with Christ in God. When Christ, who is our life, is revealed, then you also will be revealed with Him in glory." The Christian life is one of hiddenness or obscurity. Your life, my life, is hidden in God. However, this will not always be the case; obscurity will soon pass away, and our true selves will be revealed. Meanwhile, we are to seek first His kingdom and His righteousness.

In Matthew 7:7–8, Jesus says, "Ask, and it will be given to you; seek, and you will find; knock, and it will be opened to you. For everyone who asks receives, and he who seeks finds, and to him who knocks it will be opened." This promise is made to believers more than once. Deuteronomy 4:29 records the Lord's words to the nation of Israel after the Exodus: "You will seek the Lord your God, and you will find Him if you search for him with all your heart and all your soul." Again, in Jeremiah 29:13–14, God is speaking to Israel: "'You will seek Me and find Me when you search for Me with all your heart. I will be found by you,' declares the Lord." The centrality of seeking God is by no means a New Testament teaching only originating with the Gospels.

When I first studied this passage, I was taken aback by the phrase in Jeremiah 29:14: "I will be found by you," declares the Lord. It is a simple statement found in a passage talking about God's restoration of His people. At first glance, I was struck by the fact that this is a promise. Restated, the promise is, "You will find Me." I need this promise because I don't always see God or believe He is there when I'm going through difficult times. Isaiah 8:17 states what is often in our hearts: "And I will wait for the Lord who is hiding His face from the house of Jacob; I will even look eagerly for Him." Also in Isaiah 45:15: "Truly, You are a God who hides Himself, O God of Israel, Savior!" God hides Himself, and I must seek Him. In spite of my feelings and perceptions, I must learn to cling to the truth that God is near to me. I can be at rest, knowing that He is not far from me and is more concerned for my well-being than I ever will be.

For God to say I will find Him carries with it the reality that I will be found as well. The seeking and finding of God is not for His sake but for mine. In the process of seeking and finding God, I must be remade and reshaped into His likeness. God does not conform or transform to fit me as I would like to think. I will find Him, but on His terms. To learn about His terms, look to Jesus. No one gets to the Father but through Him. In many ways, Jesus is the fulfillment of the promise in Jeremiah 29:14: "You will find Me."

Everyone knows that you don't seek something that is obvious; you seek that which is hidden. God hides Himself for the very reason that we might seek Him. This is the test to see what is in our hearts. What does God's hiddenness do to you? Does it make you angry? Is it your excuse to not believe? Does it compel you to seek after Him? He hides from us (to a certain extent) to give us the chance to seek Him or to turn away.

We are not left in the dark, however, to search for a God who runs away. Just as He loved us first, He also sought us first. "Behold, I stand at the door and knock; if anyone hears My voice and opens the door, I will come in to him and will dine with him, and he with Me" (Rev. 3:20). He may hide, but He calls to us from His hiding place that we may join Him. God is patient in waiting for us. We give up so easily without instant gratification and blame God for not being where we want Him to be.

One of my favorite books is *Les Miserables* by Victor Hugo. The main character, Jean Valjean, is an ex-convict recently released from a long and unjust prison sentence. He is alone and bitter, trying to find a place to stay for the night, having been turned away at every door because no one trusts a criminal in his or her home. Finally, he is ready to give up hope, when someone approaches him:

"You have knocked at every door?" she asks.
"Yes."
"Have you knocked at that one there?"
"No."
"Knock there."[29]

He knocks at the door of a priest, who takes him in for the night. Valjean had only to knock at the right door to find acceptance. "Seek and you will find; knock and it will be opened." But the story doesn't end there. Valjean is given a good meal and a bed for the night by the kind priest. During the night, however, Valjean feels uneasy and decides to leave. He takes some of the priest's silver plates and leaves without remorse. Shortly thereafter, he is caught by some officers and brought back to the priest.

> "Ah, there you are!" said [the priest], looking toward Jean Valjean. "I am glad to see you. But I gave you the candlesticks also, which are silver like the rest, and would bring two hundred francs. Why did you not take them along with your plates?"[30]

The guards are shocked at this, as well as Valjean. The priest assures the guards that the silver had been given to Valjean and proceeds to give him the candlesticks. As the guards leave, the priest says to Valjean in a low voice:

> Forget not, never forget that you have promised me to use this silver to become an honest man.... Jean Valjean, my brother, you belong no longer to evil, but to good. It is your soul that I am buying for you. I withdrew it from dark thoughts and from the spirit of perdition, and I give it to God![31]

There are many aspects of God that are hidden from us, yet He is always pursuing us. This passage from *Les Miserables* always reminds me of the power of grace and my need for redemption *even when I don't seek it*. The priest not only showed compassion to a man who had previously stolen from others, but also he bestowed gifts on a man who stole from his own household. This is the grace of God towards me, a sinner who has offended God repeatedly and often; yet He is seeking after me and every person ever born before any of us ever have a thought of Him in our minds. My attempts to seek God are often halfhearted, if I do it at all. Yet God is there whispering, sometimes shouting, "This is the way, walk in it" (Is. 30:21). He is saying, "I know you have questions and at times wonder if I exist or where I am. I know many things are hidden from you, but take comfort, for I will be found by you."

One of my favorite passages is Deuteronomy 29:29, which says, "The secret things belong to the Lord our God, but the things revealed belong to us and to our children forever, that we may follow all the words of this law." God told Moses that if he looked fully on His glory, Moses would surely die, so God gave Moses a glimpse, which was enough. God has revealed enough of Himself to us in order that we might come to Him and be made whole, yet the mysteries of God are still numerous. However, we should be comforted by, and not fearful of, the fact that we will never come to the end of God. He will be found by those who seek Him.

This dynamic of seeking and finding is ultimately summed up in Christ. Matthew 1:21 tells us that Christ came to take away the sins of the world; He came to offer forgiveness. Often this is the last thing we seek when coming to Jesus, but it is our deepest need. When He said He would save His people, He wasn't talking about saving them from political oppression, though this is what they sought. He also wasn't talking about saving you or me from financial or relational stress, though He might work on those things in our lives. Christ sought to redeem us so that we might be found.

Forgiveness, and the desperation with which we should seek it, is beautifully brought to life in *The Tale of Despereaux*. It is the story of a heroic little mouse sent to his death by his own father for speaking to a human. Despereaux survives, and after many adventures, he returns to face his father. "Will you forgive me?" his father pleads.

> Forgiveness, reader, is, I think, something very much like hope and love, a powerful, wonderful thing. And a ridiculous thing, too. Isn't it ridiculous, after all, to think that a son could forgive his father for beating the drum that sent him to his

death? ...But still...he said, "I forgive you, Pa." And he said those words because he sensed that it was the only way to save his own heart, to stop it from breaking in two. Despereaux, reader, spoke those words to save himself.[32]

I think Christ must have felt much the same way. He was willing to forgive and pay the price for that forgiveness rather than be eternally separated from you or me. As for us, our hearts will be torn to pieces or made complete depending on whether or not we seek after Him with our whole heart, mind, and soul.

Conclusion and Reflection

What do you seek? Is it worth your life? The disciples in John 1 were looking for the Messiah, and they found Him. As a result, many of them eventually suffered imprisonments, beatings, harassments, and even death for their devotion to Christ. However, it was not in vain because they sought something beyond what this world had to offer. They sought forgiveness, purpose, hope, love, and truth. Jim Elliot, a missionary killed by cannibals, once said this: "He is no fool who gives up what he cannot keep, to gain what he cannot earn." Consider carefully what you seek.

- Is what you seek worth spending your life to obtain?
- For what or whom are you willing to sacrifice?
- In what ways do you seek the kingdom of God first in your life?
- What things keep you from seeking God first?
- What do you seek to gain from God more: forgiveness or favors?

QUESTION #9

JOHN 6:67— "YOU DO NOT WANT TO GO AWAY ALSO, DO YOU?"

> Christ came not just to give us an example of a way of life but to give us life itself. Spiritual life is not ethereal and outside us, something that we must work hard to obtain; it is in us, pervading us, as blood is in every living being.[33]
>
> —from *In His Image*

THIS QUESTION RINGS in any believer's ears at one point or another. Things get difficult, and you wonder if sticking with God is really worth it. Everyone faces hardship and pain, but the Christian is asked to believe there is a good and loving God in spite of that difficulty. As a Christian, you are required to believe that in all circumstances God is in the right. It is at those most difficult times you might hear God asking you, "Do you want to go away from Me and find your own way?" just like the Israelites whom the Lord describes in Jeremiah 2:13. They forsook the fountain of living water to dig their own wells, only to find that those wells couldn't hold water at all. When God asks this question, it's a chance to show what is truly in your heart.

Context

As with all the other questions, the context of this question is critical to understanding what Jesus was trying to accomplish. The beginning of John 6 is the account of Jesus feeding five thousand people with five loaves of bread and two fish. After witnessing this miracle, the people said, "This is truly the Prophet who is to come into the world" (6:14). The people want to set Jesus up as a political ruler or a king right then, but Jesus withdraws with His disciples. Later that evening the disciples go out to sea. A windstorm starts up and they began rowing, when suddenly Jesus is walking towards them on the water. The crowds follow Jesus and the disciples to other side of the sea.

It is at this time that Jesus turns and speaks to the people, delivering one of His most difficult teachings. It isn't difficult in the sense of trying to live it out; there are teachings more difficult in that sense (like "Love your enemies," "Pray for those that persecute you," or "Love your neighbor as yourself" [see Matthew 5–7]). This is the kind of teaching to which it was difficult to listen. It wasn't palatable to the Jews then, and it's certainly not any easier to listen to now.

In John 6:26–65 Jesus talks about bread and drink, flesh and blood, hunger and thirst, body and Spirit. Jesus criticizes the crowd for following Him for the wrong reasons: "You seek Me, not because you saw signs, but because you ate of the loaves and were filled" (6:26). The people do not want to hear teachings so they might grow closer to God; they want to see what else this Magician will produce for them. Maybe He will provide them with more food, money, or clothes.

Then there is a dialogue between Jesus and the people. I will paraphrase it:

Crowd: "What do you want us to do?"
Jesus: "Believe in the One whom God has sent."

JOHN 6:67— "YOU DO NOT WANT TO GO AWAY ALSO, DO YOU?"

Crowd: "Do a miracle (sign) so that we can see it and believe You. Our forefathers ate the manna while they were in the wilderness."

Jesus: "Moses did not give you bread from heaven; it is My Father who gives you true bread from heaven. It is the bread of God that comes down from heaven and gives life to the world."

Crowd: "Lord, we want this bread."

Jesus: "I am the bread of life; he who comes to Me will not hunger, and he who believes in Me will never thirst."

Jesus compares Himself to the manna given to the Israelites while they wandered in the wilderness for forty years. That manna was a foreshadowing of the work of Christ. Just as the bread came from heaven all those years ago to provide sustenance for a people who would otherwise have starved to death, so Christ now comes from heaven to provide salvation for a people who will otherwise be condemned. However, the Jews are not taken with this comparison. They begin grumbling among themselves, saying, "Who does this man think He is? How can He say He came from heaven?" Jesus isn't daunted by their grumbling. In fact, it seems to have spurred Him on. He becomes more graphic in His teaching about the bread. He said, "I am the living bread that came down out of heaven; if anyone eats of this bread, he will live forever; and the bread also which I will give for the life of the world is My flesh" (6:51). This causes more of a ruckus with the Jews, but Jesus keeps going:

> Unless you eat the flesh of the Son of Man and drink His blood, you have no life in yourselves. He who eats My flesh and drinks My blood has eternal life, and I will raise him up on the last day. For My flesh is true food, and My blood is true drink. He who eats My flesh and drinks My blood abides in Me, and I in him. As the living Father sent Me, and I live because of the Father, so he who eats Me, he also will live because of me. This is the bread

which came down out of heaven; not as the fathers ate and died; he who eats this bread will live forever.

—John 6:53–58

Initially, it sounds like something out of a horror movie—eating flesh and drinking blood. Who can blame the Jews for being offended at such graphic language? Anybody might find it unpleasant to listen to this teaching, but the Jews especially did. Consider the Old Testament commandments concerning blood. "Any man [an Israelite or a visitor among them]…who eats any blood, I will set My face against that person who eats blood and will cut him off from among his people. For the life of the flesh is in the blood, and I have given it to you on the altar to make atonement for your souls; for it is the blood by reason of the life that makes atonement…. As for the life of all flesh, its blood is identified with its life" (Lev. 17:10–11, 14). This is a reiteration of the covenant God made with Noah in Genesis 9:3–7. In Genesis 9:4 God commanded, "Only you shall not eat flesh with its life, that is, its blood." It was a serious offense to eat meat with the blood still in it. It was so serious, in fact, that the disciples made it one of only three things that the Gentile Christians should not do in lieu of converting to Judaism and keeping all kosher laws (see Acts 15:13–29).

The Jews in the crowd are offended, not just emotionally, but also religiously and socially. In addition, Jesus says He comes from heaven and calls Himself the Son of Man (a messianic and divine title). "As a result of this, many of His disciples withdrew and were not walking with Him anymore" (John 6:66). They stumbled over the Stumbling Block.

Digging Deeper

Why in the world would Jesus use this graphic language, knowing the audience to whom He was speaking? There are at least three reasons for Jesus to do this. First, Jesus knew their hearts, which was why He criticized them in the beginning. He knew they were following Him to see what He could do for them, not because they wanted to see the power of God. Since Jesus was not out to win any popularity contests, He deliberately used this graphic imagery to "weed out" the bad seeds. He knew His teaching would cause certain people to leave. Though He wanted to draw as many as possible to Himself, Jesus did not chase down the ones who left and try to bring them back. He let them leave and even double-checked with the ones who stayed: "Do you want to leave, too?" Those who stayed knew that it was themselves who needed to change, not the teaching (or the Teacher). My guess is that they stayed despite being slightly offended. As I stated in an earlier chapter, anyone who follows Jesus will be offended at some point.

A second reason for this teaching is that we tend to be more in tune with our physical bodies than our souls or spirits. Jesus made this powerfully graphic analogy to point out that our physical bodies are not so different from our spiritual bodies (the soul). We are more aware of our physical hunger and thirst than our spiritual hunger and thirst; however, both are valid and real. We understand that without food or water we will die a terrible death, but without Christ we will die an eternal death. Just as we take in food to nourish our bodies, so we must take in Christ to redeem our souls. Just as food sustains our bodies in this life, so Christ sustains our souls for eternity. Just as food goes to strengthen and rebuild every cell in our bodies, so Christ permeates and transforms every facet of our souls. Jesus taught that there is a more direct connection between the spiritual and physical than what we often recognize.

The third reason I see for Jesus using this analogy is simply because it was true. He fulfilled the Old Testament laws. He summed up all things related to blood, sacrifice, and redemption. When Jesus said to drink His blood and eat His flesh, it was not literal in the physical sense, but it was quite literal in the spiritual sense. Spiritually speaking, we must drink the blood of Christ and eat

His flesh. This means to take in, or consume, all of who He is. To consume is to internalize, to make it a part of our being. Christ does not desire to be some outward or distant God that we worship only in fear. He is within us, as the nutrients from food that course through our veins and throughout our bodies.

God commanded long ago that the people could not eat the blood with the meat because the blood was to symbolize redemption or atonement. Instead, the blood was poured out on the ground and thus returned to God. Many years later, Jesus told the people that they must drink His blood so that they might be redeemed. The former animal sacrifice was only another foreshadowing of the salvation that was to come. The blood of the animal could not be ingested because that would indicate that it somehow provided atonement, rather than just being a foreshadowing of Christ. The person ingesting the lifeblood (soul) would be attempting to gain salvation by taking that which belonged to God. Hebrews 10:3–4 states: "But in those sacrifices there is a *reminder of sins* year by year. For it is impossible for the blood of bulls and goats to take away sins." The sacrifices were done regularly to remind the people that blood had to be shed on behalf of their sins, but this was only a symbol of their atonement, not the real thing. "Every priest stands daily ministering and offering time after time the same sacrifices, which can never take away sins; but He, having offered one sacrifice for sins for all time, sat down at the right hand of God.... Now where there is forgiveness of these things, there is no longer any offering for sin" (Heb. 10:11–12, 18). The blood and flesh sacrifices that used to symbolize death and condemnation under the law now mean life and salvation through Christ.

Paul Brand (a missionary doctor) and Philip Yancey (a Christian author) co-wrote a book called *In His Image*. As a Christian doctor, Brand sees blood on a medical as well as spiritual level. Brand points out that we associate blood with death or injury because we typically only see it at these times. However, as a doctor and a Christian, Brand associates blood with life. He states:

> Christ came not just to give us an example of a way of life but to give us life itself. Spiritual life is not ethereal and outside us, something that we must work hard to obtain; it is in us, pervading us, as blood is in every living being.[34]

As we take in the blood of Christ, we take in His life. His blood cleanses and rejuvenates the lifeless spirit within us, just as a blood transfusion revives an injured patient.

After this difficult teaching and many people leaving, Jesus turned to His twelve disciples and asked, "You do not want to go away also, do you?" This question must be understood in the context discussed above. The teaching Jesus had just given in John 6 was not just offensive, it also was demanding and intrusive. Jesus was talking about a kind of relationship with God in which nothing is held back and nothing is off limits. The crowd wouldn't look past their offended senses to see that Jesus was offering them a connection with God that they desperately needed. Many people are comfortable with God on Sundays, at funerals or weddings, or in the occasional prayer during difficult times; but when Jesus demands more, being the jealous God that He is, we find ourselves recoiling, and He asks if we would rather leave. Many call themselves Christians, but few follow Christ. His teachings are difficult; who can accept them?

The question itself is noteworthy. The very fact that Jesus would ask something like this demonstrates a great humility. The God of creation asked this ragtag group of disciples if they wanted to leave Him. And He would have let them go if they had so chosen, just as He had let the others go. He knows that we are prone to wonder away and find our own paths. Since He desires worshipers who choose Him, He must allow for those who do not choose Him.

To be a true follower of Christ there must be at least the possibility of walking away. The problem is, where would you go if not to Christ? When a rich young man came to Jesus to inquire about eternal life, Jesus told him to sell everything and then follow Him. The young ruler was sad and went away because he was very wealthy. Jesus did not chase after Him, but He turned to the disciples and said, "How hard it is for those who are wealthy to enter the kingdom of God!" (see Luke 18:18–27 and Matthew 19:16–26). Jesus allowed the man to leave, though it did not please Him. In the light of eternity, wealth makes a poor god and an even worse savior.

Paul asks a difficult question in Galatians 4:9: "But now that you have come to know God, or rather to be known by God, how is it that you turn back again to the weak and worthless elemental things, to which you desire to be enslaved all over again?" Now that you are free, why do you desire to be a slave? Now that you have experienced the power of God, why do you turn back to weak and worthless things? Jesus let the Jews in John 6 walk away, He let the rich young man leave, and the father let his prodigal son go out into the world. God doesn't want unwilling slaves, only willing servants.

Peter gives an exemplary response to Jesus' question; it is the response of any true disciple: "Lord, to whom shall we go? You have words of eternal life. We have believed and have come to know that You are the Holy One of God" (6:68–69). Peter recognizes that though he may have felt a little put off by Jesus' words, there is no better offer anywhere else. If Jesus speaks the words of eternal life and He is the Holy One of God, then we had better listen, no matter how difficult it is.

In my darkest moments of depression or loneliness I have had those brief thoughts of leaving my faith. They are fleeting because the idea of walking away from God would not in any way be a cure for my depression or loneliness. I only think about leaving in order to show my anger toward God for not doing things the way I want.

I imagine that this would really show God that I disapprove, but it wouldn't show anything except complete foolishness on my part for leaving the only One who can do anything about my depression and loneliness. Where else would I go? There is no other hope by which I can be saved.

Hebrews 2:1 and 3 read, "So we must listen very carefully to the truth we have heard, or we may drift away from it... What makes us think that we can escape if we are indifferent to this great salvation that was announced by the Lord Jesus Himself?" Search the other world religions or deny religion altogether and you will find there is no greater salvation than what is offered through Christ. Most religions offer salvation based on works or rituals, while others dispense with the necessity for salvation completely. None of these approaches take sin seriously enough. If we say that humans are the highest good or the greatest reality, then we live a meaningless life and die a tragic death that will be soon forgotten. Man is not the measure of all things, for without God, he cannot even measure himself accurately. All people must be measured against an objective standard in order for true justice and mercy to exist.

Christianity is not just a way to salvation; it is a way of life. It is the glasses through which we see all things. C. S. Lewis was quoted as saying, "I believe in Christianity as I believe that the Sun has risen, not only because I see it, but because by it I see everything else."[35] We have spiritual eyes that see just as we have physical eyes. When I see with my spiritual eyes, I do not see the world the same as the unbeliever would. I see the world as God's creation and us as His children. I see that my circumstances are not a result of random chance but the handiwork of a Designer. Christianity changes how I look at myself, others, and God; it changes how I treat my family and how I look at the tree outside my window. There is nothing Christianity does not touch because there is nothing that God does not touch. He is an intrusive God.

This is a difficult teaching, who can accept it? Peter's answer to the question was one of submission to Jesus' authority as a child to a parent. We must realize, along with Peter, that God disciplines those He loves. As any good parent, God sets boundaries that must not be crossed and rules that should not be broken. Because of His love for His children, He has set consequences in place to deter us from sin. Hebrews 12:10–11 states:

> For they [our earthly fathers] disciplined us for a short time as seemed best to them, but He [God] disciplines us for our good, so that we may share His holiness. All discipline for a moment seems not to be joyful, but sorrowful; yet to those who have been trained by it, afterwards it yields the peaceful fruit of righteousness.

He disciplines us for our good, but at the same time asks, "Do you want to leave?" The question itself is a kind of discipline. Will you stay with Him through the most difficult times and in spite of the most difficult teachings, knowing that the reward will greatly outweigh the suffering? Will you stay, knowing that you are free to leave? Paul put it this way: "Therefore we do not lose heart, but though our outer man is decaying, yet our inner man is being renewed day by day. For momentary, light affliction is producing for us an eternal weight of glory far beyond all comparison...." (2 Cor. 4:16–17). Even maximal suffering during our time on earth will not be able to compare to the weight of glory in heaven.

Peter's answer to Jesus captures an important truth. He is saying to Jesus, what or who else is there? "You have the words of eternal life." This answer was wrought from Peter's experience thus far with Jesus. Peter wasn't claiming to understand everything Jesus taught, but he was claiming trust in the Person doing the teaching. In other words, just like Peter, you and I have excellent reasons to trust Jesus, even through the difficult times and in spite of the most difficult teachings, for He has the words of eternal life. You will search in vain to find a better way to live your life.

Conclusion and Reflection

If what you believe about God cannot be true in the darkest hours, then what good is it? You already know that God uses our suffering to teach and refine us. You also know that there is much about God that will remain hidden from us. The question is, will you remain with Him or leave?

- What happens when you must apply your intellectual knowledge of God to your practical life?
- Why is it so difficult to live out the truth of God, knowing that His ways are far better than our own?
- What things cause you to doubt God's existence, goodness, or power?
- Have you ever considered leaving Christianity? Why or why not?
- What teachings of Jesus have offended you or confused you in some way?
- Does the existence and truth of God comfort you in the midst of suffering, or does it make you angry?

If God ever asks you if you want to leave, remember Peter's response. This is salvation.

QUESTION #10

ACTS 9:4— "WHY ARE YOU PERSECUTING ME?"

> But that is the beginning of a new story—the story of the gradual renewal of a man, the story of his gradual regeneration, of his passing from one world into another, of his initiation into a new unknown life.[36]
>
> —from *Crime and Punishment*

BESIDES JESUS, THE apostle Paul is the most prominent and important figure in church history and the New Testament. He authored a significant portion of the New Testament, which is still regarded and read today as instruction for Christian living. Paul also traveled through most of Asia Minor spreading the gospel of Christ to Jews and Gentiles. In fact, Paul was the key in bridging the gap between the Jews and Gentiles in the early church. Paul's words and actions are looked upon with admiration, respect, and care, because he asked his hearers to imitate him as he imitated Christ. Christians around the world meticulously read, study, and apply his writings as they work out their salvation in fear and trembling.

Context

We know from his letters that Paul lived out a kind of reckless faith. It didn't matter what it cost him in this life, as long as the gospel was being spread and Christ was glorified. He was beaten nearly to death twice, starved, shipwrecked, imprisoned, ostracized, afflicted with physical ailments, and eventually martyred. For all this, he did not lose hope or curse God. The message of the cross compelled his ministry through the darkest times, lighting the way with its truth, purpose, and beauty. Paul never wavered in this. The call to imitate him is certainly not unfounded (2 Cor. 11:23–30; Phil. 1:12–20).

What about Paul prior to all of this? Paul the apostle was preceded by Saul the Pharisee and persecutor. Saul (his Jewish name) was a Pharisee of the tribe of Benjamin. By his own words, he was "circumcised on the eighth day, of the nation of Israel, of the tribe of Benjamin, a Hebrew of Hebrews; as to the Law, a Pharisee; as to zeal, a persecutor of the church; as to the righteousness which is in the Law, found blameless" (Phil. 3:5–6). This simply meant he had every advantage as far as his upbringing and social standing; he was from the right side of the tracks. Since he was a zealous Pharisee, Saul knew and kept every aspect of the law flawlessly. He was passionate about the law and wanted to see to it that it was never maligned or treated lightly.

The book of Acts records the beginning of the church at Pentecost, followed by Peter's sermon to the crowds in Jerusalem. Shortly thereafter, Jesus' disciples begin preaching about the resurrection and Jesus being the Messiah, and Saul is only one of the many people offended and outraged. At the end of Acts 7, Stephen, a follower of Christ, concludes his speech to the officials by claiming that they have failed to keep the law as handed down to them and have killed the prophets of God. They pick up stones to stone him to death: the execution of a blasphemer. It is Saul who watches over the executioners' robes, giving his approval of Stephen's death.

Acts 8 begins with the outbreak of persecution in the city of Jerusalem. Christians are scattered throughout Judea and Samaria, but the apostles stay in Jerusalem. As Stephen is buried, "Saul began ravaging the church, entering house after house, and dragging off men and women, he would put them in prison" (Acts 8:3). It appears that something as horrific as widespread persecution is still under the mighty hand of God, for those who scattered continued preaching the gospel. Apparently the thing intended to quench the gospel is the very thing that ensures it will spread throughout the world, for God is not without a sense of irony. This is only further proved with Saul himself.

You or I might have chosen Peter, James, or any other apostle to evangelize Asia and write the New Testament. After all, they had been with Jesus and were eyewitnesses to His miracles, teaching, resurrection, and ascension. With the empowering of the Holy Spirit, they also preached the gospel and bravely faced persecution. Saul, on the other hand, was the very kind of person whom Jesus reprimanded repeatedly. He called the Pharisees false, self-righteous, hypocritical, and deceptive (see Matthew 23). The Pharisees clung to the keeping of the law as their claim to righteousness and salvation. They held themselves in highest regard because of their exemplary adherence to the law and service to God. They did not seek forgiveness from Jesus because they did not see their own sin, and Saul was certainly no halfhearted Pharisee. Why would Saul be chosen by God rather than struck dead? For the same reason that you and I are not struck dead for our sins: God loved him and had a use for him.

Saul's transformation begins on the road to Damascus, as Luke writes in Acts 9. He is going to obtain more names of people to imprison, but before he reaches the city, a light from heaven flashes around him and he falls to the ground. Then Saul hears a voice say to him, "Saul, Saul, why are you persecuting Me?" Saul answers, "Who are You, Lord?" The voice responds, "I am Jesus whom you are persecuting, but get up and enter the city, and it will be told you what you must do" (9:1–6).

Digging Deeper

Imagine for a minute that you are a judge overseeing the case of an accused child killer. Everything about this person is repulsive to you, and all the evidence indicates that the accused is guilty; yet he maintains his innocence. You verbally threaten and abuse him to illicit a confession, but he refuses. Finally, he faces execution, and you are satisfied to see him die. Only then does the evidence come in to show that the accused was innocent after all. Imagine that moment, seeing yourself as the bearer of injustice, the very thing you took an oath to stamp out.

This is part of what Saul felt lying there on the road. Everything he had passionately worked for, the people he had killed or imprisoned—it was all based on incomplete information. Those people were telling the truth, and it was he who was in fact maligning and blaspheming against God. This was not like finding out you were wrong about something; it was like finding out you were wrong about everything.

This is what it means to meet Jesus for the first time. The truth of Jesus is not one cog in the machine, it is the machine. To be wrong about Jesus is to be wrong about everything else. However, Saul's transformation was not from black to white, or from Satan-follower to God-follower. Saul is often thought to have been a black-caped villain killing the Christians because of his hatred toward God. This is a misunderstanding of Saul, to say the least. Saul had the right pieces; they were just not fit together properly. Saul was zealous for the Lord and His purposes. He wanted to serve God, only he didn't have all the information. Saul's conversion was not from pagan to God-worshipper; rather, it was from old covenant to new covenant.

Remember that Saul was a Jew, first and foremost. From the time that the Jewish people entered the Promised Land, idolatry constantly drew them away from following the one true God. Finally, God sent judgment in the way of foreign nations coming in and destroying their cities and the temple and taking the people away as slaves. It is heartbreaking to read the account of the return of the Jews to their home many years later and the rebuilding of the temple and the city walls. The people who remembered the former glory of Solomon's temple wept bitterly for what they had lost, while cries of joy giving thanks to God also went up to the heavens (Ezra 3:10–13).

The Jews were not without struggles and difficulties after this, but there is no indication that they fell back into the worship of false gods. The horrors of the exile and the fulfilled promise of restoration cemented something in their collective conscience: God is not to be taken lightly, and He is a God of His word. This is the backdrop of Jewish monotheism—a long, painful, and ultimately redemptive history centered on a covenant between God and His chosen people. This is the history of which Saul was a zealous participant. Therefore, when Saul became aware that men and women were following after a man claiming to be God, he immediately sought to stamp them out in order to maintain a holy Jewish nation. Saul was perhaps fearful of God's judgment if he failed to eradicate this heresy.

Given this wider context of Jewish history, Jesus' question to Saul in Acts 9:4 is not condemning because under the old Law Saul was doing exactly what he should. Instead the question is redemptive, just as the other questions have been. Saul's worldview has to be restructured and rewritten with Christ at the center, holding everything together. When Jesus asks Saul, "Why are you persecuting Me?" He points out three things. First, He is indeed alive and well. Second, Jesus identifies Himself with His followers (notice He doesn't ask "why are you persecuting *My people*"). Last, Saul is the one who stood on the wrong side of the fence, not the Christians he is imprisoning. Jesus is saying, "I am the Lord, and you are fighting against Me by persecuting My followers." This message begins the long process of redemption in Saul/Paul (his Greek name).

Jesus did not fault or condemn Paul for his passion, only the direction of it. In fact, it was partly because of his passion that God called him. God knew that Paul was the sort of man who would never compromise, waver, or give in once his mind was set. The only thing left was to get his mind set right. God had created Paul with certain characteristics, which initially brought great harm to God's people. Paul was stubborn, abrasive, commanding, passionate, single-minded, and forthright. Without Jesus, Paul wreaked havoc on the followers of God, thinking he was purging the country of heresy. Once Jesus became the center, these characteristics in Paul made him the sort of man who could face suffering for the sake of the gospel that would make lesser people crumble. God speaks to Paul through a messenger, saying of Paul, "Go, for he is a chosen instrument of Mine, to bear My name before the Gentiles and kings and the sons of Israel; for I will show him how much he must suffer for My name's sake" (Acts 9:15–16). And he did suffer for the sake of Christ.

Paul's passion was wrong-headed, but Jesus did not condemn him. This is significant for us as we examine our own lives. Revelation 3:14–22 is a message from God to the church at Laodicea. God says to them, "I know your deeds, that you are neither cold nor hot; I wish that you were cold or hot. So because you are lukewarm, and neither hot nor cold, I will spit you out of My mouth.... Those whom I love, I reprove and discipline; therefore *be zealous and repent*" (3:15, 16, 19).

Consider this for a moment. God would rather you be zealous about the wrong things than be apathetic toward everything. Why? Because apathy is farther from God than evil. Evil is a twisting of the good, which means it has no existence of its own. John Mark Reynolds, a Christian philosopher, made the observation that good has no opposite, just as bread has no opposite—there is only rotten bread. Evil is rotten good, which God delights to restore. Paul was more righteous in his persecution of the church than many "Christians" today who can't be bothered to read their Bibles once in a while. God says, "Would that you hate Me or love Me, but don't act indifferent!" because hate is closer to love than indifference. I recently watched a movie that portrayed a struggling marriage and an apathetic, unfaithful husband. As he got ready to leave after being paged, the wife lamented that she would rather her husband say he hated her because at least there would be some passion in that. Hate at least desires some end result, while indifference desires nothing. Apathy is the instant death of any relationship, while the existence of hate means that some life is still there, however perilous it may be.

If I get in an argument with a friend and hurt my friend's feelings, my apathy (or hers/his) would mean we would probably never talk again. However, if I am angry or bitter enough, there is at least a chance that we will speak again; and if we were to speak again, there is also a chance that we could work things out. As long as the dialogue continues, there is hope for restoration. This is sometimes how it is in our relationship with God.

The Bible often refers to passion as hunger and thirst. Jesus says in Matthew 5:6, "Blessed are those who hunger and thirst for righteousness, for they shall be satisfied." Without the initial hunger (passion/desire), there is no satisfaction. We all "hunger and thirst," both literally and figuratively, but this is not the point that Jesus was trying to make. Everyone has a deep sense of longing, but blessed is the one who longs for *righteousness* rather than anything else. If you hunger for anything besides righteousness (which is living rightly before God) there is no promise of satisfaction, contentment, or peace.

It might follow that "cursed are those who hunger and thirst for anything besides righteousness, for they will be empty." For those who have experienced this path, it does seem like a curse. We fear admitting our hunger because we fear the outcome. The problem is not that we desire emotional gratification or peace in our relationship with God; this is good and just. God has made us to have these desires. The problem is that we expect all these benefits without living lives characterized by holiness. So what will it cost you to attain fullness? The answer is: nothing and everything. Nothing, because Christ paid the price for sin. Everything, because once you have been bought, you do not belong to yourself.

We must go back to first beatitude, "Blessed are the poor in spirit," meaning those who realize their sin and the fact that they are not capable of buying or earning their salvation. We tremble and argue, demanding our rights, wanting to preserve the self at all cost. But true humility is not the destruction or demeaning of the self; rather it is the rebuilding, the preservation, and even the foundation of its glory.

Saint Francis of Assisi was quoted as saying, "I am dying of thirst by the side of the fountain." This quote paints a realistic and tragic picture of humanity longing, searching, and in the process, dying, while the source of life is in front of them. The problem is not a lack of water but the fact that our tastes have changed. The one dying of thirst by the fountain is not thirsty for clean water, but he or she has developed a taste for salt water—a mixture that creates more thirst. We have developed tastes and passions for things which by design cannot satisfy.

There will come a time when our perceived needs and actual needs will match. At that time, we will experience the full joy of completion and contentment because we will realize for the first time that our greatest need, our deepest desire and hunger, has been met to the point of overflowing. Whether we realize it or not, redemption is our deepest hunger, and it is what we seek even in our brokenness. Do not pray for your passions to be taken away, but pray that they would be baptized and transformed so that He might receive your most intense attention and affection. This is passion with truth.

Paul had passion, but he did not have the truth (at first). Though our passion (wrong-headed or not) brings us closer to God's doorstep, it is not our salvation, however devout it might be. Passion without truth is dangerous and quickly collapses on itself, as we see with Paul.

God shows His greatness in the people He chooses for certain tasks. He chose a barren woman to bring forth a nation, a cowardly man to go before a Pharaoh, idolaters to be in the line of Christ, a shepherd boy to be a king, fishermen to be disciples, and a zealous Pharisee to be the greatest Christian evangelist who ever lived. Often God chooses people for the exact reason we would rule them out. God takes people, with all their shortcomings and failures, and uses them for His glory. It seems He delights in the impossible and unlikely. Paul's own words make this point clear in 1 Corinthians 1:26–29:

> For consider your calling, brethren, that there were not many wise according to the flesh, not many mighty, not many noble; but God has chosen the foolish things of the world to shame the wise, and God has chosen the weak things of the world to shame the things which are strong, and the base things of the world and the despised God has chosen, the things that are not, so that He may nullify the things that are, so that no man may boast before God.

Paul certainly included himself in this description, yet he was not so much taken with his sin that he couldn't see what God had for him. Paul's redemption was much like ours: lengthy, involved, and seemingly impossible. No one believed Paul at first when he claimed to be a changed man. People were skeptical, thinking that he was trying to trick them. How could it be possible that this man who was just killing and imprisoning Christians was now on their side? Stories of redemption are often that way. It takes a while to explain, and even then, it seems hardly possible.

My own experience with this involved the fear of public speaking. One day, after a particularly humiliating experience speaking in front of a small group, I went home to write in my journal. I wrote about how embarrassed I was and that I was afraid that God would make me do public speaking just because it made me so anxious. My view of God at that time led me to think that He would bring situations into my life just to humiliate me and thus keep me humble. That was more than fifteen years ago.

Through high school I did have more public speaking opportunities, and though none were very traumatic, it was still something that terrified me. College was a little bit better, and because I had to do oral presentations in just about every class, I got a lot of practice. It wasn't until my senior year, however, that things changed.

In January of 1999, I was asked to share a three to four minute testimony during a chapel service, which typically had about 700 to 800 students. I had a month to prepare…and sweat. As I prepared, though, something was different. This time I cared about what I was saying. I wanted the message to be clear to the listeners and not have them be distracted by a nervous messenger. I prayed for this, almost begging for God not to let me be nervous but to help me speak strongly. I wanted to share the things I had learned that year about God's grace to people who follow Him.

The day finally came, and God gave me exactly what I had prayed for. I was terrified until the second I drew a breath to begin speaking, and the terror suddenly went away. I shared what was on my heart and mind without breaking a sweat. I have never been more convinced of God's indwelling than I was at that very moment.

I learned three things through this experience. First, God is real, because there is no other explanation in my mind as to why I was able to do what I did. Second, God does use our weaknesses so that He can get the attention He deserves. Everyone who knew me knew that I was terrified and told me afterwards that they were amazed at what happened. Last, I learned that my focus needs to be on the message, not on the messenger (myself). Whenever I hold to this, my anxiety is kept in check.

Ironically, a few years ago I began leading a women's Bible study, and I have spoken several times in front of our church group. I don't do this begrudgingly as I once thought I would have to, rather it has become something about which I am most passionate. I have come to believe, against all apparent odds, that God does want me to be a speaker/teacher of the Bible, and it isn't something that paralyzes me anymore. It is exciting because I know that God has given me things to share and teach, and I know that He will give me the strength to do it.

This is redemption. God takes something that is deformed, useless, harmful, and frightening, and then changes it into something that reflects Him. Paul held this tension throughout his life. He never forgot his sin, and he would be the first to tell you that his was among the worst, yet he was not crippled by guilt or shame. Paul revealed more of his struggle over a physical weakness or illness in 2 Corinthians 12:7–10. God's answer to Paul was, "My grace is sufficient for you, for power is perfected in weakness" (12:9a). So Paul concluded, "When I am weak, then I am strong" (12:10b).

Jesus asked him, "Why are you persecuting Me?" In other words, "Paul, why are you on the wrong side of the fence?" Possibly one of the most shattering questions God asked of anyone, but Paul did not hide in a corner from shame or use his unworthiness as an excuse for inaction. In Paul's first letter to Timothy he wrote:

> I thank Christ Jesus our Lord, who has strengthened me, because He considered me faithful, putting me into service, even though I was formerly a blasphemer and a persecutor and a violent aggressor. Yet I was shown mercy because I acted ignorantly in unbelief; and the grace of our Lord was more than abundant, with the faith and love which are found in Christ Jesus.... Yet for this reason I found mercy, so that in me as the foremost [sinner], Jesus Christ might demonstrate His perfect patience as an example for those who would believe in Him for eternal life.
> —1 Timothy 1:12-14, 16

Truth called Paul to action, and he went. On the one hand, he was the worst of all sinners and the least of the apostles, and on the other, he instructed Christians to imitate him in his walk with Christ. It is worth repeating that the God who raises the dead can do anything. He takes the dead things and brings them to life. He takes the twisted and makes it straight. He takes ashes and makes something beautiful. We would discount anyone like Paul and say he was unworthy, but God only uses unworthy people.

One of the most powerful stories dealing with passion, guilt, and redemption is *Crime and Punishment*. It is the story of a young man who sees himself as above the law of the land. In an effort to administer his own justice, he murders an elderly pawnbroker who would often cheat him and others. Through the rest of the story he struggles with his guilt, until it nearly drives him mad. His redemption comes in his repentance and in the friendship of a young woman. In his prison cell, he picks up a Bible and begins to read it. Dostoevsky's words are profound as he describes this new beginning. It fits Paul, as well as anyone redeemed by God.

> But that is the beginning of a new story—the story of the gradual renewal of a man, the story of his gradual regeneration, of his passing from one world into another, of his initiation into a new unknown life.[37]

When Christians are "born again," it is deeper than some biological experience; it is spiritual. Biology is a story that begins with life and ends in death, but redemption is a new story that begins with the death of your self and is followed by life everlasting. Jesus explains this in a simple analogy: "Truly, truly, I say to you, unless a grain of wheat falls into the earth and dies, it remains alone; but if it dies, it bears much fruit. He who loves his life loses it, and he who hates his life in this world will keep it to life eternal" (John 12:24–25). The seed must die in order for the wheat to grow into something more useful. The question "Why are you persecuting Me?" is a call to die to yourself and get in line with Christ. It is a reminder that to be passionate and sincere is not enough; there must also be Truth, that is, the person of Christ.

Conclusion and Reflection

Passion with truth is what should characterize our Christian lives and our relationship with God. Unfortunately, we are a fickle people, prone to shallow, wrongheaded passions and half-truths. The good news is that we worship a God of truth and He is passionate about bringing us to Himself.

- In what areas is Christ calling you to align yourself with Him?
- What sin or characteristic do you see in yourself as being impossible to change?
- Do you allow your guilt over sin to cripple your usefulness to God?

- In what ways does apathy come into your spiritual life?
- How can you keep indifference from stifling your relationship with God?

In those times when it seems that God is furthest from your thoughts, turn to the psalmist's words:

> O God, You are my God; I shall *seek* You earnestly; My soul *thirsts* for You, my flesh *yearns* for You, In a dry and weary land where there is no water. Thus I have seen You in the sanctuary, To see Your power and Your glory. Because *Your loving kindness is better than life*, My lips will praise You.
>
> —Psalm 63:1–3

ENDNOTES

1. Frank Peretti, *Piercing the Darkness* (New York: Inspirational Press, 1989), 578.
2. Stephen King, *The Stand* (New York: Penguin Books, 1990), 375.
3. Frank Peretti, *Piercing the Darkness*, 578.
4. Ibid., 579.
5. C. S. Lewis, *The Voyage of the Dawn Treader* (New York: Harper Collins Publisher, 1952), 115.
6. Ibid.
7. J. I. Packer, *Knowing God* (Downers Grove, Illinois: InterVarsity Press, 1993), 154.
8. Henry F. Cary (translator), *The Divine Comedy of Dante Alighieri* (Danbury, Connecticut: Grolier Enterprises Corp, 1985), 6.
9. Ibid.
10. Ibid., 4
11. Kenneth Grahame, *The Wind in the Willows* (New York: Henry Holt and Company, 1980), 108.
12. Alvin Plantinga, *God, Freedom, and Evil* (Grand Rapids, Michigan: William B. Eerdman's Publishing, 1974), 29–34.

13. Kenneth Grahame, *The Wind in the Willows*, 108.
14. Philip Yancey, *Reaching for the Invisible God* (Grand Rapids, Michigan: Zondervan Publishing , 2000), 27.
15. Lee Strobel, *The Case for Faith* (Grand Rapids, Michigan: Zondervan Publishing House, 2000), 50.
16. G. K. Chesterton, *Orthodoxy* (Colorado Springs, Colorado: Waterbrook Press , 2001), 229.
17. Ibid.
18. Anne Graham-Lotz, *Just Give Me Jesus* (Nashville, Tennessee: Word Publishing, 2000), 4.
19. G. K. Chesterton, quoted in *The Jesus I Never Knew* by Philip Yancey (Grand Rapids, Michigan: Zondervan Publishing House, 1995), 12.
20. C.S. Lewis, *Mere Christianity* (San Francisco: Harper Collins Publishers, 2001), 47–65.
21. Anne Graham-Lotz, *Just Give Me Jesus*, 4.
22. http://watchmannee.org
23. Yancey, *The Jesus I Never Knew*, 17.
24. Benjamin Jowett (translator), *The Dialogues of Plato* (New York: Liveright Publishing Corp, 1927), 123.
25. C. S. Lewis, *Til We Have Faces* (San Diego: Harcourt Brace and Company, 1956), 294.
26. Benjamin Jowett (translator), *The Dialogues of Plato*, 123.
27. C. S. Lewis, *The Horse and His Boy* (New York: Harper Collins Publishers, 1954), 161–162.
28. Victor Hugo, *Les Miserables* (New York: Washington Square Press, 1966), 10.
29. Ibid.
30. Ibid, 29.
31. Ibid, 30.
32. Kate DiCamillo, *The Tale of Despereaux* (Cambridge, Massachusetts: Candlewick Press, 2003), 207–208.

33. Paul Brand and Philip Yancey, *In His Image* (Grand Rapids, Michigan: Zondervan Publishing House, 1987), 69.
34. Ibid.
35. C. S. Lewis, quoted in *Bruce & Stan's Guide to Cults, Religions, & Spiritual Beliefs* by Bruce Bickel and Stan Jantz (Eugene, Oregon: Harvest House Publishers, 2002), 19.
36. Fyodor Dostoevsky, *Crime and Punishment* (New York: Bantam Books, 1986), 472.
37. Ibid.

BIBLIOGRAPHY

Bickel, Bruce and Stan Jantz. *Bruce & Stan's Guide to Cults, Religions, & Spiritual Beliefs*. Eugene, Oregon: Harvest House Publishers, 2002.

Brand, Dr. Paul and Philip Yancey. *In His Image*. Grand Rapids, Michigan: Zondervan Publishing House, 1987.

Cary, Henry F. (translator). *The Divine Comedy of Dante Alighieri*. Danbury, Connecticut: Grolier Enterprises Corp, 1985.

Chesterton, G. K. *Orthodoxy*. Colorado Springs, Colorado: Waterbrook Press, 2001.

DiCamillo, Kate. *The Tale of Despereaux*. Cambridge, Massachusetts: Candlewick Press, 2003.

Dostoevsky, Fyodor. *Crime and Punishment*. New York: Bantam Books, 1987.

Graham Lotz, Anne. *Just Give Me Jesus*. Nashville, Tennessee: Word Publishing, 2000.

Grahame, Kenneth. *The Wind in the Willows*. New York: Henry Holt and Company, 1980.

Hugo, Victor. *Les Miserables*. New York: Washington Square Press, 1966.

Jowett, Benjamin (translator). *The Dialogues of Plato*. Edited by W.C. Greene. New York: Liveright Publishing Corp, 1927.

King, Stephen. *The Stand*. New York: Penguin Books, 1990.

Lewis, C.S. *Mere Christianity*. San Francisco: Harper Collins Publishers, 2001.

———. *The Voyage of the Dawn Treader*. New York: Harper Collins Publishers, 1952.

———. *The Horse and His Boy*. New York: Harper Collins Publishers, 1954.

———. *Til We Have Faces*. San Diego: Harcourt Brace and Company, 1956.

———. *The Problem of Pain*. New York: Macmillan Publishing Company, 1962.

Packer, J. I. *Knowing God*. Downers Grove, Illinois: InterVarsity Press, 1993.

Peretti, Frank E. *Piercing the Darkness*. New York: Inspirational Press, 1989.

Plantinga, Alvin. *God, Freedom, and Evil*. Grand Rapids, Michigan: William B. Eerdman's Publishing, 1974.

Strobel, Lee. *The Case for Faith*. Grand Rapids, Michigan: Zondervan Publishing House, 2000.

Yancey, Philip. *The Jesus I Never Knew*. Grand Rapids, Michigan: Zondervan Publishing House, 1995.

———. *Reaching for the Invisible God*. Grand Rapids, Michigan: Zondervan Publishing House, 2000.

To order additional copies of this book call:
1-877-421-READ (7323)
or please visit our Web site at
www.WinePressbooks.com

If you enjoyed this quality custom-published book,
drop by our Web site for more books and information.

www.winepressgroup.com
"Your partner in custom publishing."

LaVergne, TN USA
07 April 2011
223305LV00001B/60/P